Reviewed by the
Parent-Teacher Advisory Board

Developmental Overview by Nancy Richard

becker & mayer!
BOOKS

A FIRESIDE BOOK
Published by Simon & Schuster

JENNIFER RICHARD JACOBSON
and DOTTIE RAYMER

How Is My *Second Grader* Doing in School?

WHAT TO EXPECT AND HOW TO HELP

FIRESIDE
Rockefeller Center
1230 Avenue of the Americas
New York, NY 10020

becker & mayer!
BOOKS

Produced by becker&mayer!
www.beckermayer.com

BOOK DESIGNED BY BARBARA MARKS

Assessment booklet designed by Heidi Baughman
Interior illustrations by Cary Pillo, Mat Hatnak, and Dan Minnick
becker&mayer! art director: Simon Sung
becker&mayer! editor: Jennifer Worick

Manufactured in the United States of America

3 5 7 9 10 8 6 4 2

The Library of Congress has catalogued the Simon & Schuster edition as follows:
Jacobson, Jennifer, date.
    How is my second grader doing in school? : what to expect and how to
help / by Jennifer Richard Jacobson, Dottie Raymer.
        p.   cm.
    Includes bibliographical references and index.
    1. Second grade (Education)—United States.   2. Education, Primary—
Parent participation—United States.   3. Parent-teacher relationships—
United States.   4. Language arts (Primary)—United States.   5. Mathe-
matics—Study and teaching (Primary)—United States.   I. Raymer, Dottie.
II. Title.
LB1571.2ndJ33   1998
372.24'1—dc21   98-17855
                                                                             CIP

ISBN 0-684-84710-8
0-684-85439-2 (Pbk)

Acknowledgments

We would like to give special thanks to Nancy Richard, who wrote the Developmental Overview for this book. Nancy has studied child development, school readiness, and effective classroom practices for the past thirty years. As a consultant on the national lecture staff of the Gesell Institute of Human Development and a consulting teacher for the Northeast Foundation for Children, she has worked with thousands of teachers and parents throughout the country to promote classrooms that are educationally successful as well as responsive to the developmental needs of children. She coauthored *One Piece of the Puzzle: A School Readiness Manual.*

In addition, we would like to thank the members of our Parent-Teacher Advisory Board who volunteered countless hours to reading and evaluating the books in this series. They have graciously shared their knowledge and insight. Their wisdom, gathered through years of working with children in classrooms, has enriched these books tremendously. Their guidance has been invaluable. Members of the Parent-Teacher Advisory Board are as follows:

Jim Grant, a former teacher and principal, is an internationally known consultant and one of America's most passionate advocates for children. He is the founder of the Society for Developmental Education, the nation's primary provider of staff development training for elementary teachers. He is also founder and co–executive director of the National Alliance of Multiage Educators. He is the author of dozens of professional articles and educational materials; his books—*"I Hate School!" Some Common Sense Answers for Educators and Parents Who Want to Know Why and What to Do About It, Retention and Its Prevention,* and *A Common Sense Guide to Multiage Practices*—are recognized resources for teachers, parents, and administrators.

Mary Mercer Krogness, a public school teacher for over thirty years, is the recipient of the Martha Holden Jennings Master Teacher Award, the highest recognition the foundation bestows on a classroom teacher in Cleveland, Ohio. She has taught grades k-8 in both urban and suburban schools and is currently a language arts consultant for five school systems, an educational speaker, and an author. In addition to award-winning articles, Mary has written *Just Teach Me, Mrs. K: Talking, Reading, and Writing with Resistant Adolescent Learners,* and she was the writer-producer of an award-winning, nationally disseminated PBS television series: *Tyger, Tyger, Burning Bright,* a creative writing program for elementary age students.

Nancy O'Rourke, an early childhood specialist, has been a teacher for sixteen years. Most recently, she has taught in a first and second grade multiage classroom. Well recognized for her contributions to her Maine school system, Nancy has served on the early childhood task force, developed math and science curricula, and helped create school-wide benchmarks for grades k–3 in math, science, and the humanities. Nancy also brings her experience as a parent of two school-age children to her role as adviser.

Robert "Chip" Wood is the cofounder of the Northeast Foundation for Children, a nonprofit educational foundation whose mission is to improve education in elementary and middle schools. The foundation provides training, consultation, and professional development opportunities for teachers and administrators. It also operates a k–8 laboratory school for children and publishes articles and books written by teachers for educators and parents. Chip has served NEFC as a classroom teacher, consultant, and executive director. He is the author of many professional articles and the book *Yardsticks: Children in the Classroom, Ages 4–14* and coauthor of *A Notebook for Teachers: Making Changes in the Elementary Curriculum.*

We would like to thank the talented staff at becker & mayer, who produced this book, especially Jim Becker, who offered this idea; Andy Mayer, who has followed it through; Jennifer Worick, who graciously navigated this book through all channels; Simon Sung, who coordinated the art; Heidi Baughman, who designed the assessment booklet; Jennifer Doyle, who worked with panel members; Dan Minnick, who drew computer sketches; and Kelly Skudlarick, who worked on the original proposal.

We would also like to acknowledge the members of the Simon & Schuster publishing group, particularly Trish Todd, who has shared our vision and commitment to this series; Cherise Grant, who has been engaged in all aspects of production; Barbara Marks, who designed the book; Toni Rachiele, the production editor; and Marcela Landres who did a little bit of everything.

And finally we would like to thank the countless teachers, parents, and children who have offered their knowledge, anecdotes, insights, artwork, and advice. We hope you recognize your contributions on these pages.

For Dottie—J.R.J.

For Willie and Elsie—D.E.R.

Contents

How Is My Second Grader Doing In School?

Introduction

Phew! You are now the parent of a second grader. This year your child probably knows the ropes. She knows how to arrive at school, how long the school day will be, where to go for lunch, and what will happen if she loses a tooth in the middle of math class. Perhaps you are feeling some relief. Your guidance and support are not nearly as necessary as they were when your child entered kindergarten or first grade. Or are they?

Most schools report a drop in parent participation when children reach the second grade. Sometimes parents have the impression—and sometimes schools give the impression—that second grade is the time for parents to relinquish their educational responsibility. Nothing could be farther from the truth.

Studies for over three decades have concluded that parent involvement in a child's education—that is, throughout a child's educational career—is a leading contributor to academic success. Children from all socioeconomic backgrounds are happier, are more motivated, and get better grades when their parents take an active role in helping them to learn. You know your child better than anyone else does. You know what interests and motivates her, how she learns best. You were your child's first teacher. You are still her most important teacher. This is no time to hand your child over to "the system." Even if her school and teachers are exceptional, her most influential learning environment is still her home. And if the school or teacher is not all you might have hoped for, your child still needs to know that her education is important to you. Children benefit most when parents and teachers work as partners.

This book is intended to help you do what you do best—use your knowledge of and interest in your child to help her grow and flourish. It will inform you of the concepts and skills taught in second grade. It will help you determine what your child knows, what she needs to know next, and what she wants to know. It will also give you more ideas than you can possibly use for supporting your child in an enjoyable and relaxed manner.

In the front of the book you will find an observational assessment. The observational assessment has three components: the For Kids Only booklet found in the envelope at the back of this book, the Parent Observation Pages, on page 35, and the Assessment Guide, on page 55, and is divided into three parts: Reading Assessment, Math Assessment, and Writing Assessment. Assessments are often controversial. On the basis of one assessment, a child might be labeled "gifted" in one town. That same child might then move to another town, take a different assessment, and no longer qualify for the gifted and talented program. In other words, different assessments often come up with different results. Or assessments developed to measure one thing, such as IQ, actually measure something else, such as a child's prior knowledge. The assessment in this book has been designed for one purpose only: *to help you to help your child.* To ensure the very best results in gathering information, please read "How to Use This Book," page 31, before you begin the assessment.

The observational assessment will help you introduce to your child ideas, skills, and concepts that are sequentially appropriate. For instance, if you try to teach your child how to add or subtract two-digit numbers before she has a solid understanding of place value, you may actually hinder rather than help her mathematical understanding. The observational assessment can help you determine how well your second grader grasps the concepts. It will also direct you to the appropriate activities to reinforce those concepts.

The thought of teaching your child at home may be daunting. After all, you and your child probably have more than enough obligations to fill your time already. However, supporting your child's academic progress at home does not necessarily mean establishing a separate teaching time. It is more a matter of using the time you already have in a more stimulating, productive, and creative way. By discovering your child's strengths and weaknesses, you can capitalize on the time that you *do* have together.

One way of helping your child is to practice responding with questions rather than giving answers. By simply asking a question that helps your child think about a problem, you can provide insight, practice, or reinforcement. If your second grader asks, "How many more days until we go to Uncle John's?" you might answer, "How can we find that out?" Perhaps your child will suggest counting back on a calendar, subtracting one date from another, or using a mental strategy such as this: "Well, there are three days until Saturday, and you said we're going two weeks from Saturday. Since a week has seven days, and seven plus seven is fourteen, I guess we're going in seventeen days." By asking a question, you've taken advantage of what teachers call a teachable moment. You'll find that most of the activities in this book take less than five minutes and can help you capture those valuable moments.

As with all the books in this series, the learning activities in *How Is My Second Grader Doing in School?* cover the broad strokes of the second grade reading, writing, and math curricula. Science, social studies, the arts, and physical education are not covered because the content in these subjects varies drastically from school to school. Nevertheless, they are essential to a sound education, and your child needs to know that you value these subjects as well. Find out what your child is studying in these areas and see if there is a way you can contribute. Explore new knowledge in science and social studies. Go to museums and attend concerts and plays with your child. Most of all, let your child see that you are a learner, too.

Developmental Overview

by Nancy Richard

Ah, the second grader. Quiet and contemplative. Sober and serious. Does this sound like anyone you know? Perhaps and perhaps not. It is important to remember that in any grade, children will range in age, and that even within that age, each child has an individual rate of growth as well as an individual pattern of growth. Some children grow fast; others, more slowly. All children in the second grade will not be exactly alike, nor will they learn in the same way. Every child is unique. Because of school laws, however, most second graders will be seven to eight years old at the beginning of the school year and eight to eight and a half at the end. The curriculum of second grade is geared toward children of this age, and the behavior of this age sets the tone for the classroom. Good teachers at this age level understand and work with the difficulties of the age, but they also use the strengths of the age to help children learn.

Intellectual Prowess

Unlike their carefree and rather careless first grade selves, second graders are thinkers and analyzers. When you ask, "How did you get that answer?" a second grader will answer, "I did it in my head," or "My brain just told me," or "I figured it out."

Seven- to eight-year-olds reveal a new and deeper intellectual dimension: the ability to reflect on things, reach conclusions, and find logical solutions. They love categorizing animals, bugs, fish, and even rocks, which they never seem to tire of collecting. They love learning anything new: magic, science, experimenting. They're curious about how things work. They ponder, consider, and weigh things. On casual observance, this may look like idle daydreaming, but it is really thoughtful reflection, a new and powerful tool for problem-solving.

Language

While second graders are talkers, and some are so dependent on conversation that they seem to talk all day long, they are also listeners and, especially, questioners. They are interested in the precision of language. They want to say things just right and want others to say things right also. You may find your second grader correcting your use of language. Consider this a sign of his newly acquired intellectual prowess. You may also notice his use of lots of adjectives as well as an expanded vocabulary of adverbs such as "unfortunately" and "definitely."

If you listen carefully, you'll hear another new development in your second grader's language: the use of words like "upside down" and "sideways." His mind is now capable of turning things around, of indicating a shift in position. When he was younger, a cup was simply a cup whether it was upside down or not, but at seven to eight years old he will name it with precision: "an upside-down cup." This same ability to shift things in his mind shows up in the second grader's ability to identify left and right on another person. He can now understand and deal with opposites. In mathematics, this new ability enables him to comprehend subtraction, to count backwards, and to work with simple equations.

On the not-so-bright side, the language of seven- to eight-year-old children is also riddled with negativity and expressions of inadequacy: "I can't. I quit. The teacher didn't show me how. We haven't had that yet. I don't like it." This negativity is connected to the not-so-sunny emotional makeup of the second grader. At around seven to eight years of age, most children go through an introspective, fearful stage of disequilibrium, or imbalance.

Emotions

You will be impressed with your second grader's newfound maturity this year. After the exuberance of first grade, your seven- to eight-year-old's quiet perseverance and thoughtfulness will be welcome. Second graders can be moody, sulky and self-conscious, however. They may complain they have no friends, that you favor their siblings, or that you pick on them. They may complain that the teacher doesn't like them and doesn't treat them fairly. They may cry over the slightest criticism or over a real or imagined slight or meanness on another's part. In addition to crying, children at this age often release their tension by biting their fingernails, twisting their hair, and chewing on their collars and sleeves. They incessantly fiddle with anything at hand—a pencil, an eraser, a stone, or a bottle cap. They seem to need to be surrounded by things. They take things to the table, take things to bed, and take everything they can stuff into their backpacks to school.

As a parent, you may need to develop a new touch. Humor, superficial praise, and exaggerated affection, which were so successful in first grade, are not welcome now. The wacky teasing that delighted your first grader can be devastating to the sensitive second grader. Keep in mind that your child is not trying to be difficult. Sulking and complaining are simply characteristic of the age. Let your child know that you are on his side.

Worries and Fears

Children of this age are worriers. At school, they worry that their work will not be good enough, that they won't have time to finish, or that they'll make a mistake and be ridiculed. They worry that nobody likes them, that the other kids will make fun of them, that they'll have no one to play with. You can help your second grader to feel emotionally safer by discussing these concerns openly. "What would happen if you make a mistake?" "What could you do if you don't understand how to start your work?" "What would you do if you couldn't find a friend at recess?"

Second graders are curious about death and are worried about all the possible causes. In school, they write about death, especially under the guise of the death of pets or other animals. They are usually concerned not about their own death but about yours. Second graders are very family-oriented. What they really need to know is who would take care of them if you weren't around.

Parents are sometimes surprised at how much second graders worry about things that are happening in the world. With TV in everyone's living room, the world is small. Second graders can worry about war, famine, the ozone layer, or AIDS. This is probably a good year to limit, or at least monitor, television viewing.

You probably remember a time in your child's preschool years when he was afraid of monsters, especially of monsters in his bedroom. Perhaps you acknowledged those fears and bought some "monster spray." Or perhaps you put a sign on the door: No Monsters Allowed! Maybe you bought your child a stuffed animal that scared monsters away, or told him about his guardian angel, who would protect him against monsters.

Many fears of seven- to eight-year-olds are just as irrational as those preschool fears. You still need to acknowledge the fear. However, instead of brushing or pretending the fear away, try to give your child a way of confronting it. If you second grader is fretting about the plight of dolphins, show him how to write to the World Wildlife Federation or Greenpeace for information about ways he can help. If he's obsessing about pictures he has seen of starving children, help him contact Oxfam International or UNICEF. Give your anxious second grader a way to feel that he can make a difference. If night fears return, as they often do, create a soothing bedtime routine.

Writing about fears is one of the ways children can work them out. Other ways are available through art, drama, and especially free play. Free play is underestimated in its contribution to healthy development. Free play reinforces children's social, organizational, and physical skills and emotional well-being. Free play is also probably the single best arena in which children can flex their creative and intellectual muscles.

Encourage free play by limiting the amount of time your child spends in front of the television and the computer. Let your child have time to be bored. Don't jump in with suggestions. Provide props, such as dress-up clothes, large crates, and junk from a yard sale. One second grader designed and sewed hats for all her friends, using a box of felt given to her by a neighbor. A stethoscope or some Band-Aids will help a child work out a fear of going to the hospital.

Privacy and Sociability

Second graders are much more settled down in school than they were in first grade. While they'll sometimes work in a group, they prefer to work with one other child or alone, using their own implements at their own desks. They will write their names on anything allowed, establishing their right of ownership. They tend to be loners, and they often create a privacy shield by piling up their books around their working area. This is probably a good strategy, since they are easily distracted.

At home they try to find a quiet corner, a room or place of their own. They need a place to keep their things protected from younger brothers and sisters. You often find the seven- to eight-year-old reading under a table or making a tent on the bed in order to establish some privacy for reading or rumination.

Second graders are extremely sensitive to the feelings and attitudes of others, but they often lack social graces of their own. Major pastimes are tattling, alibiing, and blaming. According to them, someone is always being mean to them. The problem is that friendships shift very quickly at this age. Often the best friend today is the worst enemy tomorrow. It is a good idea for teachers and parents to avoid getting caught up in these squabbles and to help the child think of what might work better next time. The chances are things will look quite different to the child tomorrow. This advice, of course, does not pertain to any abusive acts, which do need immediate intervention by adults.

An especially distressful event that begins in second grade and continues into third, and one that does need intervention by teachers and parents, is the exclusion of certain children by others and the formation of clubs. Clubs are really cliques, which are forerunners of middle school behavior. The "who's in, who's out" behavior involved in forming clubs is very hurtful to the child who is left out, and it does not encourage empathy on the part of the insiders. It is a hard lesson to learn that those children who are "inside" today may be "outside" tomorrow.

Perfectionism

Second graders do love to work, but a quality that both helps and hinders them in this endeavor is the need to be correct, the need to be right, the need to be perfect. This perfectionism comes out in many ways. They do things over and over again, trying to get them right. And do they use those erasers! With their heads and eyes way down and close to their work, they write, erase, write, erase, write, erase. They often wear holes in their papers, which they tape up in exasperation, striving for a quality in their work that always seems to elude them. You can help them strive for *one* kind of perfection when they are writing: either correct spelling *or* correct punctuation *or* good handwriting, but not more than one at a time.

The Sense of Time and the Need for Closure

Most second graders have difficulty orienting themselves in time. They are just beginning to feel the sense of how long something will take, but they have no real grasp on it. At the same time they have an obsession with finishing everything: their reading, their TV program, their homework. If a definite ending place has not been established for them, they tend to go on and on until they are exhausted and cranky. For this reason, transitions from one chore to another can be tricky, and your child may need your assistance.

It is helpful if you establish some kind of closure for your child—for example, "Read three pages in your book tonight," or "Your writing for today will be finished after you've done four sentences." Simple reminders about chores are helpful, too: "We'll eat dinner right after your TV program," or "When your homework is in your backpack, you can take your bath." One advantage of books written on a second grade level is that they provide a stopping place at the end of each chapter.

To help them keep oriented in time, second graders like schedules. They like to know what's going to happen during the day or the week. Even if the schedule isn't adhered to, the plan is comforting. Some second graders like marking off days on the calendar. Others like to make lists of things to do and cross off items as they complete them.

Because of this difficulty with time, second graders are afraid morning after morning that they will be late for school. A predictable morning routine will help, as will your assurance that you will get your child to school or to the bus stop on time. If your child walks to school, you may want to tell him what time he will have to leave home each day and show him that time on a clock.

Learning

A sense of achievement is very important to second graders. They know when they've succeeded, when a job is well done. They don't like the shallow praise that first graders thrive on, but they do need your encouragement. When working with your child, choose one thing to comment on in a positive and encouraging manner. You might say, for instance, "I especially like all the bright colors you used in your painting," or "Those subtraction problems you're doing look hard." Faber and Mazlish's book, *How to Talk So Kids Will Listen*, has an excellent explanation of the difference between praise and encouragement.

The vision of the second grader may be narrowly focused. They often pull things closer to their eyes in an attempt to figure them out. In fact, they often look nearsighted as they work with their heads at an angle, practically lying on top of their papers and desks. Because of their increased absorption in close work, second graders tire easily and need alternating periods of more physical activity. If you notice your second grader rubbing his eyes or blinking, or even if you see his muscles trembling, it is probably nothing to worry about. These are common outlets for the tension of children of this age, especially after an extended period of close work. However, if you notice that your child consistently has difficulty seeing the television screen or road signs, do consult your pediatrician. If your child is expected to copy from the blackboard at school and is having difficulty, make sure you speak with the teacher. This task is too hard for most second graders. Even though many will make an admirable stab at it, most children can't make the visual shift from near to far vision and back again that is necessary to this process.

Most of those young characteristics that are seen in kindergarten or first grade, such as making letters from the bottom up, and making numbers and letters backwards, are naturally worked out by the middle of second grade. If your child is still displaying any of these characteristics, it is the time to determine whether it indicates overall youngness or if there is a learning problem that can be solved or at least compensated for. This is especially important if reading is not coming along as expected. If your child is having difficulty with academics at any time during the second grade year, don't hesitate to check with the teacher.

Questions and Answers About Second Grade

Will my child's second grade classroom look like her first grade classroom?

If your child is in the same school as last year, the structure of her classroom this year probably won't be wildly different from last year's. Indeed, many schools combine their first and second grades to give teachers more flexibility in addressing the wide range of abilities found in this age group. That being said, different teachers have different teaching styles that are bound to be reflected in the classroom environment. One teacher may feel that privacy-loving second graders work best at individual desks. Another may believe that learning is more active and collaborative when the work is done at tables or even on the floor. Still another may use a blend of both approaches. If you look closely, however, you will find that all good second grade classrooms share common elements:

- Learning is active and hands-on. Children work with lots of concrete materials (counters, blocks, movable letters or word cards) and tools (maps, rulers, thermometers).
- Children are involved in a variety of activities. Good teachers approach concepts from many different angles and allow their students to respond in whatever way best suits their strengths and interests.
- Concepts are connected to each other and to the children's world.
- Education does not happen only in the classroom. A strong second grade program encourages the active involvement of both parents and the community.

My child is still struggling with "We Can Read" books while her best friend reads chapter books with ease. Should I be concerned?

Educators agree that reading proficiency develops sometime during the first three years of school (four, if you count kindergarten). However, readiness for reading, like the rest of your child's development, operates within its own time frame. You may be surprised—and relieved—to learn that there is a wide range of "normal" reading abilities in second grade. Listen to your child read. Is she able to sound out or recognize by sight more words than she could a couple of months ago? If you are seeing steady progress, chances are your child is right on target for what she is developmentally ready to do.

My child's teacher used the whole-language approach to reading last year, but this year my child is still struggling with reading. Isn't it time to get down to business? What ever happened to basic phonics?

First, let's define some terms. "Whole language" refers to a teaching approach that stresses reading for meaning within the context of good literature. "Phonics" methods teach children to blend letter sounds to decode words in a structured, sequenced manner. These two methods of teaching reading are not—indeed, should not be—mutually exclusive. A good program provides children with a variety of literature and teaches all sorts of strategies, including phonics, for unlocking the meaning of words. Do not be misled by a lack of worksheets and lengthy phonics lessons. Many teachers prefer to teach decoding skills like phonics in mini-lessons or as individual needs arise. Remember, children progress at different rates. The best way to ease your mind is to visit your child's classroom and observe what is happening there.

My child's writing is filled with spelling mistakes. Why doesn't the teacher correct them?

Your child is probably being encouraged to use practice spelling (sometimes called transition or invented spelling). Learning to spell, like learning to speak, progresses in a predictable manner. The practice spellings that you may see in your child's writing are approximations—an important step in the process of learning to write and to use conventional spellings. Chances are, you will begin to see a great change in your child's spelling habits this year. She will begin to ask for the "book" spellings or the "real" spellings of words. She will need strategies to help her find correct spellings. She might use a dictionary, a spelling list, or the spell-check function on the computer, for example. If your child is not showing an interest in moving from transitional spelling to conventional spelling by the middle of the second grade, talk to her teacher. It may be time to step in and evaluate her progress.

All my child seems to do during math time is play with blocks and counters.
When is she going to learn to solve problems on paper?

Second grade is a transitional year in math. Especially at the beginning of the year, second graders need concrete objects like cubes or counters to work out their math problems. Look for a gradual shift as the second grade progresses, however. For many children, the need for concrete objects to figure things out is replaced by mental figuring. When this occurs, they love oral challenges—for instance, "How much is two plus five minus one?"

If you are doing pencil-and-paper work with your child in math, it may help you to know a couple of common second grade stumbling blocks. Too many math examples on a workbook page can cause your second grader, who is striving for accuracy and perfection, a great deal of distress. In this situation, fewer examples are better. Divide the work on the page into portions to be done in separate sittings. You also may run into trouble if addition and subtraction are mixed together on the same page. Since the second grade mind has difficulty with quick transitions, it's better to keep one kind of operation on a page. If this is not possible, try putting check marks next to similar problems so that your child can do like problems in a group.

My child already knows how to carry and borrow (called regrouping or
trading in most classrooms), and she complains about being bored in
math. Should I ask the teacher to give her more work?

Be careful whenever you hear the word "bored." It doesn't always mean what you think it does. Second graders who say they are bored are often telling you that they are uncomfortable or anxious. It could be that your child knows the arithmetic procedures of carrying and borrowing but doesn't really understand why she carries the one or borrows the ten. If her teacher is approaching math from a problem-solving perspective, your child might not know how to apply her skills to the problem at hand. She is caught in an "I know it, but I don't *know* it" bind: she knows the trick ("I'm smart"), but she doesn't know how to use it when she needs to ("I must be dumb"). Give her lots of opportunities to solve real-life problems at home (see page 162 for activities). If she seems comfortable with both the computation and the problem-solving, then talk with her teacher about adjusting the program to meet her needs.

How can I help my child with homework?

Teacher's attitudes toward homework vary greatly. If you have a concern about the amount of homework your child is or is not receiving, request a meeting with the teacher. Remember that young children need unstructured time to explore, discover, and imagine on their own as well. Also, always try to set aside a brief time to read with your child. Even ten minutes of daily reading is priceless time spent with your child, both academically and personally.

My child's teacher talks a lot about learning styles and multiple intelligences. What does she mean?

Educational buzzwords come and go. One year everyone's talking about integrated curriculum, and the next year they're talking about dimensions of learning. To a parent, this jargon can make the process of educating a child sound much like programming a computer.

There is, however, more value to educational jargon than meets the eye (or ear). Look at the information below. Each of the terms tells about how children learn. Teachers who pay close attention to how their students learn can adapt their programs accordingly and give their students a greater chance for success. Parents who understand how their child learns can be more sympathetic with the frustrations the child faces in school and more helpful in finding alternative approaches. At the very least, parents need to know how to talk to teachers about their child. Some of the current terms are defined below. Remember, these classifications are not meant to label or pigeonhole children; rather they are an attempt to understand how individuals learn best. Though you or your child may prefer one approach or another, most of us have a bit of each style within us.

Learning Styles

Imagine asking for directions at a gas station. The attendant tells you, "Go about a half mile down to County Route B, then turn left onto County Route W. Go about five miles until you come to the crossroads of Routes 116 and 47. Don't turn there. Keep going until you hit Highway 8. That's where you want to turn." If you caught all that, you are definitely an *auditory learner*. If, on the other hand, you cried, "Wait! Show me on a map!" you probably learn better *visually*. There are three main learning styles:

- *Auditory learners learn by listening.* If you show this kind of learner the fact 6 + 6 = 12 written on a page, it probably doesn't mean a lot. But if you chant it, it will be in her head for life.
- *Visual learners learn by seeing.* This kind of learner needs to see to believe. Draw six stars and six more stars on paper so that she can get a picture in her head.
- *Kinesthetic, or tactile, learners learn by moving their bodies or by touching.* Have this kind of learner build a six-block tower and add another six blocks right on top. If the tower holds up, she'll know her fact.

Multiple Intelligences

In the book *Frames of Mind: The Theory of Multiple Intelligences* (Basic Books), Dr. Howard Gardner describes eight ways in which people learn or approach problems. From this work has come the statement, "What matters is not how smart you are, it's how you are smart." To teach a class the addition fact 6 + 6 = 12, a teacher might offer a variety of tasks that take advantage of each type of intelligence. The eight intelligences described by Dr. Gardner and appropriate tasks for each are listed below. How are *you* smart?

- *Linguistic intelligence* is the ability to use and understand language in all its forms. Write a story about the addition fact.
- *Logical-mathematical intelligence* is the ability to use numbers and math concepts. Use pennies to show the fact.
- *Visual-spatial intelligence* is the ability to understand the relationships of images and figures in space. Draw a picture to show the fact.
- *Musical-rhythmic intelligence* is the ability to hear tone and pitch and to sense rhythm. Make up a rhyme or song about the fact.
- *Bodily-kinesthetic intelligence* is the ability to move with grace and strength. Hop along a number line to show the fact.
- *Interpersonal intelligence* is the ability to work with other people and lead them. Work with a partner to come up with a way to show the fact.
- *Intrapersonal intelligence* is the ability to understand one's own emotions, motivations, and goals. Think of a time when knowing the fact might come in handy in your own life.
- *Naturalist intelligence* is the ability to understand things that exist in the natural world. Find an example of the fact in nature.

For more information about these educational theories, look for these books in your library:

- *Emotional Intelligence,* by Daniel Goleman (Bantam)
- *How Your Child Is Smart,* by Dawna Markova (Conary Press)
- *In Their Own Way: Discovering and Encouraging Your Child's Personal Learning Style,* by Thomas Armstrong (J. P. Tarcher)
- *Nurture by Nature,* by Paul D. Tieger and Barbara Barron-Tieger (Little, Brown)
- *Seven Pathways of Learning: Teaching Students and Parents about Multiple Intelligences,* by David Lazear (Zephyr Press)
- *Unicorns Are Real,* by Barbara Meister Vitale (Warner)

How to Use This Book

Using the observational assessment

Assessment is a natural process for parents. Every time you asked your young child a question—"Can you say, Dada?" "Where is your nose?" "What color is this?"—you were collecting information and using the information to determine what to teach your child next. If you had questions about your child's development, you asked your pediatrician or consulted a checklist of developmental stages of learning. By observing your child and asking the right questions, you were able to support your child's learning.

Now that your child is school-aged, however, you may find it harder to maintain the role of supportive coach. It's a greater challenge to get a clear understanding of what is expected of your child. Without specific knowledge of the curriculum, you may not know what questions to ask. The purpose of this book, and of the accompanying assessment, is to help you to observe your child with awareness again.

The word "assessment" comes from roots that mean "to sit beside." The informal assessment is a way for you to sit beside your child and collect the information you need. After you have observed your child, you will be guided to activities that will encourage you and your child to continue to learn together.

Remember, the assessment is not a standardized test. It will not tell you how your child compares to other children in the nation. It will not even tell you how your child compares with your neighbor's child. But it will give you a starting point for determining how to increase your child's confidence and success in learning. Instructions for participating in the assessment are as follows:

1. **Take the For Kids Only booklet out of the envelope in the back of the book and read through it one time.** This will familiarize you with the visuals that you will be presenting to your child. Cut out the coins and ruler on the back cover of the booklet. Gather 25 counters (beans, coins, paper clips, etc.).

2. **Photocopy and read the Parent Observation Pages (page 35).** Reading these pages ahead of time will help you to see how the child booklet and your instructions are coordinated. It will also allow you to decide how much of the assessment you want to give to your child at one sitting. Even if you think your child will be able to respond to most of these questions, it is recommended that you give the three parts of the assessment (math, writing, and reading) at different times. You may even decide to divide the three parts into even smaller sections to suit your child's attention span or your particular time schedule.

3. **Provide a place to give the assessment that is relatively free of distractions.** Talk to your second grader about the activities. Tell your child that you want to learn more about him and that these activities will teach *you*. Make sure you approach the activity in a lighthearted manner.

4. **Above all, keep the assessment fun and relaxed for your child.** If your child is afraid to try an activity, don't push him. After all, that is valuable information for you, too. Whenever your child has difficulty with a reading passage or a math problem, *stop* and skip ahead to the question your Parent Observation Pages recommend. There is never a reason to work beyond your child's comfort level.

5. **Give positive reinforcement as often as possible.** You might say, "I didn't know you could do that!" or "When did you get so smart?" If your child seems upset or confused by an exercise, let him off the hook. You might say, "That question is confusing, isn't it?" Make sure your child ends the assessment feeling successful. One way of doing this is to return to a question your child can answer with obvious ease. Say, "I forgot to write your answer down. Can you show me how you did this problem again?"

Using the Assessment Guide

The Assessment Guide (page 55) will allow you to find out what your child knows and what he is ready to learn next. If you find that a question on the assessment did not give you enough information or if you are confused about your child's response, you may want to talk to your child's teacher. (See page 175 for more information.)

Using the Suggested Activities

In each skill area, activities are suggested under two headings: "Have Five Minutes?" and "Have More Time?" Some of the activities in the five-minute section are quick games that you and your child can play while waiting for dinner, riding in the car, or walking to the bus stop. Others are activities that you can explain in less than five minutes and then let your child complete on his own. Activities in the "Have More Time?" category do require more planning or a longer time commitment on your part.

Do not feel that you should do every activity listed under a skill heading. A number of different activities are provided so you can pick and choose the ones that appeal to you and your child. And don't feel guilty if you haven't tried something new for a while. If you do only a couple of these activities occasionally, you will be giving your second grader a genuine boost toward success. You'll be amazed at how a question here, a three-minute activity there, can demonstrate to your child how much you value his ideas and his education. Feel free to adapt these activities to your needs.

Even if you are not directed to a specific section, you may want to try some of the activities in that section. Reviewing has wonderful benefits. When your child revisits a skill, he usually gains a deeper understanding that he can apply to new learning. In every area there are sure to be games that your child will enjoy playing.

Should you pursue activities that seem more difficult? Probably not. Pushing your child too fast may backfire. Instead of looking forward to the games you initiate, your child may associate them with confusion, boredom, or failure. It's good to remember that success is the greatest motivator of all.

Some of the activities are competitive. Some second grade children do not like competitive games and cannot handle them gracefully. If your child is one, make the activity noncompetitive. Rather than playing against each other, make yourselves a team and try to beat the clock or another imaginary player—who always makes foolish decisions!

Reassess

Repeat the assessment when appropriate.

After some time has gone by—perhaps two or three months—and you and your child have participated in many of the activities, you may want to give the assessment, or a portion of it, again. By reassessing, you can determine if your child has grown in his understanding of concepts. It's possible that the

Assessment Guide (page 55) will direct you to new areas of learning to focus on next.

If you choose not to give the entire assessment a second time, make sure you ask some questions that you know your child will answer competently. *Always end the assessment on a positive note.*

Remember, the assessment is meant to be an informal tool for gathering information. You may want to adapt the questions or ask new questions to see if your second grader has truly mastered a skill.

Many teachers now assess children in the classroom by doing what one educator, Yetta Goodman, termed kid watching. This is what parents have always done best. Have a ball watching your child grasp new knowledge.

Parent Observation Pages

Photocopy the Parent Observation Pages. This will allow you to match your child's responses to the answer guide more easily. It will also allow you to repeat the assessment with your child or to give the assessment to a sibling.

Ask your child the questions in italics that appear throughout the assessment. Do not feel, however, that you must rigidly adhere to the wording here. These questions are meant to be a guide, not a script. You may find other ways of questioning that are more suited to your own and your child's needs. For more information, see How to Use This Book, page 31.

Reading Assessment

Use assessment booklet pages 2–3 for questions 1–3.

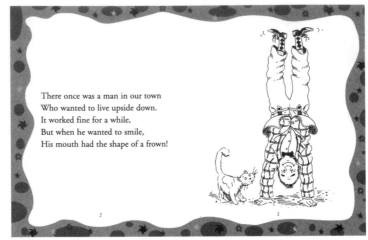

There once was a man in our town
Who wanted to live upside down.
It worked fine for a while,
But when he wanted to smile,
His mouth had the shape of a frown!

1. **Use pages 2–3 of the booklet.** Ask your child, *Can you read this poem?* If your child stops at a word, give him or her a moment to figure it out. If necessary, supply the word and encourage your child to continue.
Circle the words your child has difficulty reading.
There once was a man in our town
Who wanted to live upside down.
It worked fine for a while,
But when he wanted to smile,
His mouth had the shape of a frown!
___ None

2. What does your child do to figure out a word he or she doesn't know? Check all that apply.
___ Sounds it out
___ Guesses based on context
___ Skips the word and then goes back
___ Looks at the picture
___ Knew all the words

3. Can your child answer these questions? Check all **correct** answers.
___ A. *How did the man want to live?* (upside down)
___ B. *What happened when he tried to smile?* (He frowned.)
___ C. *Why did his mouth have the shape of a frown?* (A frown is an upside-down smile.)

If your child stopped at 5 or more words in the poem, *stop here* and go to question 13.

Use assessment booklet pages 4–5 for questions 4 and 5.

___ D. *Would you like to live upside down? Why or why not?* (Check if your child gave a response to the question.)

4. **Use pages 4–5 of the booklet.** If your child stopped at fewer than 5 words, ask, *Can you read this story?* If your child stops at a word, give him or her a moment to figure it out. If necessary, supply the word and encourage your child to continue.
   Circle the words your child has difficulty reading.

   Kirby hopped out of bed the minute he heard the alarm. He put on a pair of jeans and a shirt. Then he quickly made his bed. Next, he ran to the bathroom to wash his face and comb his hair. He raced down to the kitchen and poured himself a bowl of cereal. Kirby's dad came into the kitchen.
   "Surprise!" yelled Kirby. "I'm all ready for school!" Kirby's dad smiled and pointed to the calendar on the wall. "Oh, no!" Kirby moaned. "I forgot what day it is!"
   ___ None

5. What does your child do to figure out a word he or she doesn't know? Check all that apply.
   ___ Sounds it out

___ Divides it into parts or syllables
___ Guesses based on context
___ Skips the word and then goes back
___ Looks at the picture
___ Knew all the words

6. Can your child answer these questions? Check all **correct** answers.
   ___ A. *What was Kirby doing in this story?* (He was getting ready for school.)
   ___ B. *What did Kirby do first?* (He hopped out of bed.)
   ___ C. *What did Kirby do after he raced downstairs?* (He poured some cereal.)
   ___ D. *What was Kirby's mistake?* (He forgot it was Saturday.)
   ___ E. *What do you think Kirby will do next?* (Check if your child tries to answer the question.)

> **I**f your child stopped at 5 or more words in the previous story, *stop here* and go to question 13.

Use assessment booklet pages 6–7 for questions 7–9.

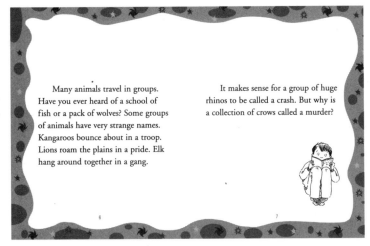

Many animals travel in groups. Have you ever heard of a school of fish or a pack of wolves? Some groups of animals have very strange names. Kangaroos bounce about in a troop. Lions roam the plains in a pride. Elk hang around together in a gang.

It makes sense for a group of huge rhinos to be called a crash. But why is a collection of crows called a murder?

7. **Use pages 6–7 of the booklet.** If your child stopped at fewer than 5 words, ask, *Can you read this story?* If your child stops at a word, give him

or her a moment to figure it out. If necessary, supply the word and
encourage your child to continue.
Circle the words your child has difficulty reading.

    Many animals travel in groups. Have you ever heard of a school of fish
or a pack of wolves? Some groups of animals have very strange names.
Kangaroos bounce about in a troop. Lions roam the plains in a pride. Elks
hang around together in a gang. It makes sense for a group of huge rhinos
to be called a crash. But why is a collection of crows called a murder?
___ None

8. What does your child do to figure out a word he or she doesn't know?
Check all that apply.
    ___ Sounds it out
    ___ Divides it into parts or syllables
    ___ Guesses based on context
    ___ Skips the word and then goes back
    ___ Knew all the words

9. Can your child answer these questions? Check all **correct** answers.
    ___ A. *What is the story about?* (groups of animals)
    ___ B. *In the sentence "Lions roam the plains in a pride," what does the
    word "pride" mean?* (group)
    ___ C. *Can you remember any of the group names mentioned in the story?
    Which ones?* (school of fish, pack of wolves, troop of kangaroos, pride
    of lions, gang of elks, crash of rhinos, murder of crows)
    ___ D. *Think of a group of animals that you like. What would be a good
    name for the group?* (Check if your child responds to the question.)

If your child stopped at 5 or more words in the story above, *stop here* and
go to question 13.

*Use assessment
booklet pages 8–9
for questions
10–12.*

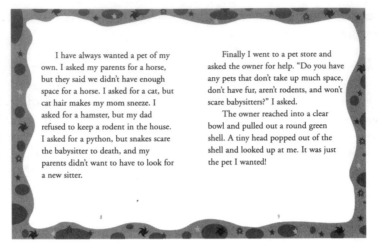

10. **Use pages 8–9 of the booklet.** If your child stopped at fewer than 5 words, ask, *Can you read this story?* If your child stops at a word, give him or her a moment to figure it out. If necessary, supply the word and encourage your child to continue.

Circle the words your child has difficulty reading.

I have always wanted a pet of my own. I asked my parents for a horse, but they said we didn't have enough space for a horse. I asked for a cat, but cat hair makes my mom sneeze. I asked for a hamster, but my dad refused to keep a rodent in the house. I asked for a python, but snakes scare the baby-sitter to death, and my parents didn't want to have to look for a new sitter.

Finally I went to a pet store and asked the owner for help. "Do you have any pets that don't take up much space, don't have fur, aren't rodents, and won't scare baby-sitters?" I asked.

The owner reached into a clear bowl and pulled out a round green shell. A tiny head popped out of the shell and looked up at me. It was just the pet I needed!

___ None

11. What does your child do to figure out a word he or she doesn't know?
Check all that apply.
___ Sounds it out
___ Divides it into parts or syllables
___ Guesses based on context
___ Skips the word and then goes back
___ Knew all the words

12. Can your child answer these questions? Check all **correct** answers.
___ A. *What does the kid in the story want to have?* (a pet)
___ B. *Why couldn't the kid have a cat?* (Cat hair made the child's mom
sneeze.)
___ C. *What is a python?* (a snake)
___ D. *Do you think the kid could have a pet mouse? Why or why not?* (no,
because it is a rodent, like a hamster)
___ E. *What kind of pet did the store owner show the kid?* (a turtle)
___ F. *Can you think of any other pets the child might be able to have?*
(Check if your child's answer fits the restrictions given in the story.
Answers might include hermit crabs, fish, frogs, or lizards.)

13. Which of the passages can your child read fluently (in smooth, expressive
phrases rather than choppy individual words)? Check any that apply.
___ None
___ poem
___ Saturday story
___ animal groups story
___ pet story

Check any that apply:
___ Consistently reads fluently
___ Reads lines fluently but sometimes loses the place between lines
___ Reads word by word rather than in phrases
___ Frequently stumbles or stops to figure out words

Math Assessment

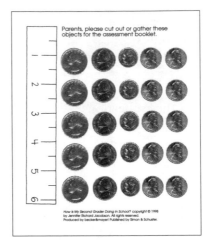

Before beginning the math assessment, cut out the coins and ruler on the back cover of the assessment booklet. Collect 25 small items—pennies, for example, or paper clips, beans, stones, or bits of torn paper—to use as counters. Have paper and pencil available for your child to use. You may also wish to have a watch with a second hand.

1. Count out 25 counters. Then say to your child, *Can you organize the counters so that a friend could tell how many there are without counting one by one?* Next, say, *Can you find another way to organize them?* Check one.

    ___ Can find one way to organize the counters into groups—for example, five groups of 5, or two groups of 10 and one group of 5

    ___ Can find at least two ways to organize the counters into groups

    ___ Cannot organize the counters into groups at this time

10

100

1000

14, ___, 16, 17, ___, ___, 20

45, 46, 47, ___, ___, ___, 51

838, ___, ___, ___, 842, 843, 844

1000, ___, ___, ___, ___, 1005, 1006

57, 56, ___, 54, 53, ___, ___

second, third, ___, fifth, ___, ___

10   11

Use assessment booklet pages 10–11 for questions 2 and 3.

2. **Use page 10 of the booklet.** *I'm going to ask you some questions. Point to the number that makes the most sense.*
   - *Which number shows* about *how many shoelace holes are in a sneaker?* (10)
   - *Which number shows* about *how many leaves are on a tree in summer?* (1,000)
   - *Which number shows* about *how many pages are in a chapter book?* (100)
   Check all that apply.
   ___ Points correctly to 10
   ___ Points correctly to 100
   ___ Points correctly to 1000
   ___ Cannot point correctly to any of the numbers at this time

3. **Use page 11.** Say, *Can you tell what numbers are missing?*
   If necessary, point to the numbers in each row and help your child read them aloud. Circle **incorrect** responses. (Correct responses are underlined.)
   14, <u>15</u>, 16, 17, <u>18</u>, <u>19</u>, 20
   45, 46, 47, <u>48</u>, <u>49</u>, <u>50</u>, 51
   838, <u>839</u>, <u>840</u>, <u>841</u>, 842, 843, 844
   1000, <u>1001</u>, <u>1002</u>, <u>1003</u>, <u>1004</u>, 1005, 1006
   57, 56, <u>55</u>, 54, 53, <u>52</u>, <u>51</u>
   second, third, <u>fourth</u>, fifth, <u>sixth</u>, <u>seventh</u>

4. *Can you count by:*

Twos?	Yes, to ____	Not at this time ___
Fives?	Yes, to ____	Not at this time ___
Tens?	Yes, to ____	Not at this time ___
Threes?	Yes, to ____	Not at this time ___

5. **Use page 12.** *Can you tell me if this number is even?*
   Point to each number. Circle **incorrect** responses.

   2   6   11   22   33   70   102   205   756   998

Use assessment booklet pages 12–13 for questions 5 and 6.

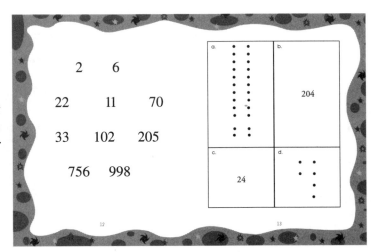

6. **Use page 13 in the booklet.** *Which of these shows the number twenty-four? Can you find another one?*
   Circle the letters of the boxes your child points to.
   a.   b.   c.   d.

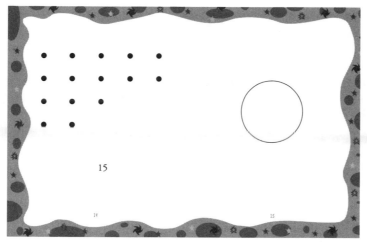

*Use assessment
booklet pages
14–15 for
questions 7 and 8.*

7. **Use page 14 of the booklet.** Point to the number 15. Then ask:
   What does the 5 mean in this number? Can you circle that many counters?
   What does the 1 mean in this number? Can you circle that many counters?
   Circle all that apply.
   ___ Can circle five counters to show the meaning of the 5 in 15
   ___ Cannot show the meaning of the 5 at this time
   ___ Can circle ten counters to show the meaning of the 1 in 15
   ___ Cannot show the meaning of the 1 at this time

8. **Use page 15.** Hand your child the ten cut-out pennies. *Guess about how
   many pennies will fit in this circle.*
   Have your child guess. Then use the pennies to check the guess.
   Your child's guess _____
   Actual number _____

9. *Guess about how many giant steps it would take for you to get across this
   room.*
   Choose any appropriate starting and ending place. Have your child
   guess, then take giant steps to check the guess.
   Your child's guess _____
   Actual number _____

10. *Here are some problems for you to do in your head. See how fast you can give me the answers.*

    Read aloud the problems below, without the answers. Use the second hand on a watch or stopwatch, or silently count "one Mississippi, two Mississippi . . ." to time your child on each problem. Check each response that takes longer than 5 seconds. Circle incorrect answers.

  a $6 + 2 = 8$
  b. $4 + 9 = 13$
  c. $8 + 7 = 15$
  d. $7 + 5 = 12$
  e. $8 + 5 = 13$
  f. $7 + 3 = 10$
  g. $3 + 5 = 8$
  h. $9 + 9 = 18$

    Talk briefly about strategies your child used to find the answers, particularly to those answered correctly but not within 5 seconds. Two possible strategies are "I counted up from six," and "I know that seven plus seven equals fourteen, so I added one." Note any strategies your child mentions.

11. *Here are some problems for you to do in your head. See how fast you can give me the answers.*

    Follow the procedure used in problem 10. Check each response that takes longer than 5 seconds. Circle incorrect answers.

  a. $9 - 4 = 5$
  b. $10 - 6 = 4$
  c. $17 - 8 = 9$
  d. $13 - 6 = 7$
  e. $12 - 5 = 7$
  f. $18 - 9 = 9$
  g. $7 - 2 = 5$
  h. $17 - 7 = 10$

    Talk briefly about strategies your child used to find the answers, particularly to those answered correctly but not within 5 seconds—for example, "I counted back from ten" or "I know that four plus five equals nine, so nine minus four must be five." Note any strategies your child mentions.

26	180	65	277		47	467	82	500
+23	+215	+16	+115		-22	-152	-19	-123

Show or tell how you got each answer.

Show or tell how you got each answer.

16

17

Use assessment booklet pages 16–17 for questions 12 and 13.

12. **Use page 16 in the booklet.** *Can you solve these problems?*

Copy the following problems, without the answers, on a sheet of paper or have your child solve the problems in the For Kids Only booklet. Circle incorrect answers.

a. 26	b. 180	c. 65	d. 277
+ 23	+ 215	+ 16	+ 115
49	395	81	392

Talk briefly about strategies your child used to find the answers—for instance, "I added the ones first and then the tens," or "I added the tens." Note any strategies your child mentions.

13. **Use page 17.** *Can you solve these problems?*

Copy these problems, without answers, on a sheet of paper or have your child solve the problems in the For Kids Only booklet. Circle incorrect answers.

a. 47	b. 467	c. 82	d. 500
– 22	– 152	– 19	– 123
25	315	63	377

Talk briefly about strategies your child used to find the answers, such as "I know that 19 is one less than 20, so I did 82 – 20 = 62 and then added one to the answer." Note any strategies your child mentions.

14. *Can you show me 35¢ with the coins?*
Can you show me 35¢ another way?

   Give your child the punch-out coins. Repeat the procedure and check your child's response:

   35¢ ___ one way ___ two ways
   58¢ ___ one way ___ two ways
   $1.40 ___ one way ___ two ways

Use assessment booklet pages 18–19 for questions 15 and 16.

MENU

Muffin . . . . .50¢

Milk . . . . .35¢

Juice . . . . .20¢

Orange or Apple . . . . . . .10¢

Butter . . . . .2¢

18

a. You want a muffin, butter, and milk. How much will it cost?

b. You want two muffins and a glass of juice. How much will it cost?

c. You have two quarters and you buy some milk. How much money do you have left over?

19

15. **Use pages 18–19 in the booklet.** *Look at this menu. Can you solve these problems?*

   If necessary, read the problems aloud to your child. Have cutout coins and paper and pencil available. Circle **incorrect** answers.
   a. *You want a muffin, butter, and milk. How much will it cost? (87¢)*
   b. *You want two muffins and a glass of juice. How much will it cost? ($1.20)*
   c. *You have two quarters and you buy some milk. How much money do you have left over? (15¢)*

16. **Use page 18.** *Can you use the menu to make up a problem of your own? How would you solve that problem?* Check one.
   ___ Can make up problem and explain how to solve it
   ___ Can make up problem but cannot explain how to solve it
   ___ Makes up problem, but doesn't use information in menu
   ___ Cannot make up a problem a this time

Use assessment booklet pages 20–21 for questions 17 and 18.

17. **Use pages 20–21 in the booklet.** *Look at this clock. Can you tell me what time it shows?*
Point to each clock face. Circle **incorrect** responses.
7:00   2:30   8:15   5:40

18. **Use page 20.** Point to the first clock (7:00). Check all **correct** responses.
Look at this clock. What time will it be
___ *an hour from now?* (8:00)
___ *a half hour from now?* (7:30)
___ *fifteen minutes from now?* (7:15)
___ *How much time has gone by since 5:00?* (two hours)

If your child answered each of the above questions correctly, repeat the procedure using one of the other clock faces.

*Use assessment
booklet pages
22–23 for
questions 19
and 20.*

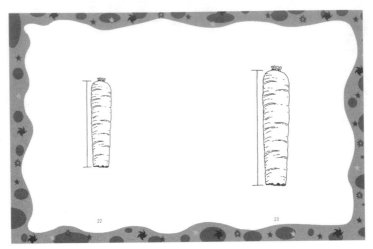

19. **Use page 22 in the booklet.** *Use the pennies. Can you tell me about how long the carrot is in pennies?* Check one.
    ___ Yes (4 pennies)
    ___ Not at this time

20. **Use page 23.** *Use the ruler. Can you tell me how long the carrot is in inches?* Check all that apply.
    ___ Yes (4 inches)
    ___ Not at this time

*Use assessment
booklet pages
24–25 for
questions 21
and 22.*

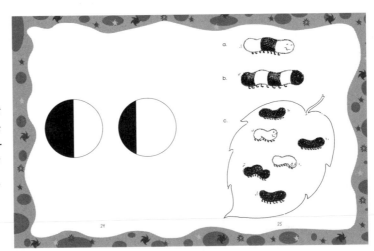

21. **Use page 24 in the booklet.** *Which picture shows one half?* Check one.
    ___ First picture (correct response)
    ___ Second picture (incorrect response)
    ___ Both pictures (incorrect response)
    ___ Neither picture (incorrect response)

22. **Use page 25.** *Name the part that is shaded.* Check all **correct** responses.
    ___ a. (1/3)
    ___ b. (3/5)
    ___ c. (4/6 or 2/3)
    ___ d. No correct answers at this time

23. *Can you draw a picture that shows one-fourth?*
    Have your child draw a picture on a sheet of paper. Check one.
    ___ a. Drawing shows four approximately equal parts with one part
        shaded. (correct response)
    ___ b. Drawing shows four very unequal parts with one part shaded.
    ___ c. Drawing shows four parts, but an incorrect number of parts are
        shaded.
    ___ d. Drawing shows more or fewer than four parts.
    ___ e. Cannot make a drawing at this time

24. Have your child draw the following shapes on a sheet of paper. Check all
    correct responses.
    Can you draw
    ___ *a circle?*
    ___ *a rectangle?*
    ___ *a diamond?*
    ___ *an oval?*

Use assessment booklet pages 26–27 for questions 25 and 26.

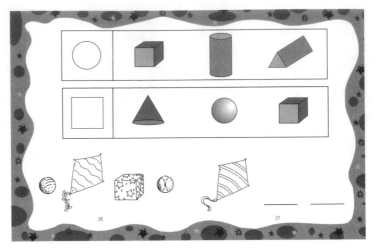

25. **Use pages 26–27 in the booklet.**
Point to the circle. *Which of these objects could help you draw this shape?* (cylinder)
Point to the square. *Which of these objects could help you draw this shape?* (cube)
Check all that apply.
___ Points correctly to cylinder
___ Points correctly to cube
___ Cannot point to the correct shapes at this time

26. **Use pages 26–27.** *Look at this pattern. Can you tell me what the next two shapes would be?* (box, ball) Check one.
___ Yes
___ Not at this time

27. *Here are seven counters. Can you give me an addition or subtraction problem for seven?* If necessary, use the following prompt: *For example, if I had ten counters, I could make the addition sentence 5 + 5 = 10.*
Can you give me another addition or subtraction sentence? Check one.
___ Can make one sentence
___ Can make two or more different sentences
___ Cannot make a sentence at this time

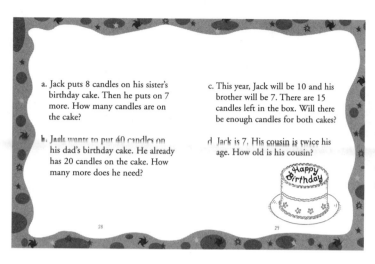

a. Jack puts 8 candles on his sister's birthday cake. Then he puts on 7 more. How many candles are on the cake?

b. Jack wants to put 40 candles on his dad's birthday cake. He already has 20 candles on the cake. How many more does he need?

c. This year, Jack will be 10 and his brother will be 7. There are 15 candles left in the box. Will there be enough candles for both cakes?

d. Jack is 7. His cousin is twice his age. How old is his cousin?

Use assessment booklet pages 28–29 for questions 28 and 29.

28. **Use pages 28–29 in the booklet.** *Can you solve these problems?*
    If necessary, read the problems aloud to your child. Have counters and paper and pencil available. Circle **incorrect** answers.
    a. *Jack puts eight candles on his sister's birthday cake. Then he puts on seven more. How many candles are on the cake?* (15)
    b. *Jack wants to put forty candles on his dad's birthday cake. He already has twenty candles on the cake. How many more does he need?* (20)
    c. *This year, Jack will be ten and his brother will be seven. There are fifteen candles left in the box. Will there be enough candles for both cakes?* (no)
    d. *Jack is seven. His cousin is twice his age. How old is his cousin?* (14)

29. What strategies did your child use to solve the problems? Check all that apply.
    ___ Used counters or other objects
    ___ Drew a picture
    ___ Acted it out
    ___ Made a list
    ___ Looked for a pattern
    ___ Guessed and checked

Use assessment booklet page 30 for question 30.

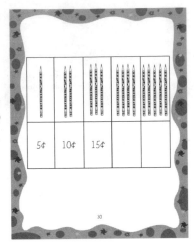

30. **Use page 30 in the booklet.** *Can you tell me what numbers are missing in this chart?* Check **correct** responses.
      ___ 20¢ (4 pencils)
      ___ 25¢ (5 pencils)

Writing Assessment

Write about a time when someone you know was very naughty.

Give your child a sheet of lined paper and a pencil. This will provide you with one writing sample. Does your child's writing sample show the following? Check all that apply.
      ___ Expresses ideas clearly and in logical sequence
      ___ Expresses ideas but incompletely or in random order
      ___ Writes more than one complete sentence
      ___ Uses capitalization and punctuation properly
      ___ Uses conventional spellings most of the time
      ___ Uses practice spellings most of the time
      ___ Can tell or draw story but will not write one

Assessment Guide

This assessment guide will tell you the meaning of the data you collected during the parent observation. It will also direct you to the activity sections in the book that are most appropriate for *your* second grader.

Reading Assessment

Over the years, the methods by which children have been taught to read have changed. You may have been taught to sound the word out. Your father may have been taught to memorize words by sight. Educators now know that children need many strategies to make sense of the printed word. Good readers

- make predictions based on what they already know
- use clues from illustrations or graphics
- use the context to figure out unfamiliar words
- use letter sounds (phonics) to decode words
- recognize words by sight

To be a proficient reader, your child, too, must learn to use different strategies in a flexible manner. A reader who tries to figure out words based solely on context clues may find it difficult to move beyond predictable picture books.

On the other hand, a reader who tries to sound out every word is apt to lack fluency or recite words without understanding the meaning behind them. The Reading Assessment will help you determine which skills and strategies your second grader has already acquired and which ones, with strengthening, will help him or her grow into a flexible, competent reader.

Question 1

Some of the words in this poem are sight words that are used frequently and should be instantly recognized. Others are words that can be decoded by sounding them out (phonics), breaking them into parts (word structure), or predicting the meaning from the text (context clues).

See the Sight Word activities on page 98 if your child had difficulty with any of the following words: there, once, was, a, in, who, wanted, to, live, for, but, when, he, his, had, of.

Use the Phonics activities on page 83 and the Word Study exercises on page 92 if your child had difficulty with these words: man, our, town, wanted, upside, down, worked, fine, while, smile, mouth, shape, frown.

Question 2

This question will help you determine which strategies your child is using to decode words. He or she should be comfortable using two or more strategies. If your child is relying on only one strategy, or if the strategies he or she uses don't seem to be working, see Phonics, page 83; Word Study, page 92; and Reading Comprehension, page 66. If your child could read this passage with ease, questions 3 to 12 will give you additional opportunities to record strategies.

Question 3

These questions help you to determine whether or not your child understands what he or she reads.

Questions A and B check your child's ability to recall what is stated in the text.

Question C asks your child to use picture clues and to infer meaning from the text.

Question D encourages your child to use critical thinking skills to synthesize the information in the text and apply it to his or her own life.

If your child could read the words, but had difficulty answering any of these questions, see Reading Comprehension, page 66. If your child particularly enjoyed answering Question D, see Reading and Writing Enrichment, page 117, for activities that will support and enhance your child's reading and writing.

Question 4

See the Sight Word activities, page 98, if your child had difficulty with any of these words: out, of, the, minute, he, heard, put, on, a, and, then, his, to, wash, poured, himself, into, surprise, I'm, all, ready, for, school, oh, no, I, what, it, is.

See Phonics, page 83, and Word Study, page 92, if your child had difficulty with these words: *Kirby, hopped, bed, alarm, pair, jeans, shirt, quickly, made, next, ran, bathroom, face, comb, hair, raced, down, kitchen, bowl, cereal, Kirby's, dad, came, yelled, smiled, pointed, calendar, well, moaned, forgot, day.*

Question 5

Watch carefully when your child stumbles upon an unknown word. If your child is using the same strategy over and over, or if the strategy he or she is using isn't working, see Phonics, page 83; Word Study, page 92; and Reading Comprehension, page 66. If your child could read the story with ease, questions 6 to 12 will give you additional opportunities to record strategies.

Question 6

These questions help you determine whether your child understands what he or she reads.

Question A asks your child to tell the main idea of the story.

Questions B and C check your child's ability to recall a sequence of events.

Question D requires your child to draw a conclusion based on the information provided in the text and in picture clues.

Question E asks your child to predict what will happen next.

If your child could read the words but had difficulty answering any of these questions, see Reading Comprehension, page 66. If your child particularly enjoyed answering Question E, see Reading and Writing Enrichment, page 117, for activities that will support and enhance your child's reading and writing.

Questions 7–8

Note which words cause your child difficulty and what he or she does when faced with an unknown word. If your child is using the same strategy over and over, or if the strategy he or she is using isn't working, see Phonics, page 83; Word Study, page 92; and Reading Comprehension, page 66.

Question 9

Here is another opportunity to check your child's comprehension.

Question A asks your child to summarize what he or she has read.

Question B checks your child's understanding of the vocabulary.

Question C checks your child's ability to recall some details of what he or she has read.

Question D encourages your child to apply what he or she has read to new situations.

If your child had difficulty answering one or more of the questions, see Reading Comprehension, page 66. If your child particularly enjoyed answering question D, see Reading and Writing Enrichment, page 117, for activities that will support and enhance your child's reading and writing.

Questions 10–11

Note which words cause your child difficulty and what he or she does when faced with an unknown word. If your child is using the same strategy over and over, or if the strategy he or she is using isn't working, see Phonics, page 83; Word Study, page 92; and Reading Comprehension, page 66.

Question 12

These questions check your child's literal and critical comprehension.

Question A asks your child to state the main idea of the story.

Question B checks your child's understanding of cause-and-effect relationships.

Question C checks your child's understanding of vocabulary.

Question D asks your child to make comparisons.

Question E requires your child to use clues in the text to draw a conclusion.

Question F requires your child to evaluate information.

If your child had difficulty answering one or more of the questions, see Reading Comprehension, page 66. If your child is able to read and understand all of the passages with ease, you may wish to repeat the above activities with a book that is slightly more difficult than the ones your child generally reads. See also the activities in Reading and Writing Enrichment, page 117.

Question 13

If your child reads slowly, word for word, or has difficulty keeping his or her place while reading, see Fluency, page 101.

Math Assessment

Competency in mathematics involves more than getting the right answer to a computation problem. A child might be able to solve 53¢ + 36¢ on paper and still not be able to tell you if a dollar is enough money for a 53¢ pen and a 36¢ pencil. To be mathematically literate in today's world, your child must be able to use mathematical ideas and computation skills to solve the complex problems that pop up in everyday life. Along with basic computation skills, your child must know how to approach unfamiliar problems, how to figure out what needs to be done, and how to decide if the end result is reasonable.

Assessing these skills goes beyond marking answers right or wrong. To find out how your child is really doing in math, you must watch carefully as he or she goes about the business of solving a problem. The questions on the Parent Observation Pages will help you begin a habit of close observation so that you can help your child learn the mathematical thinking that today's world demands.

Question 1

Many of the mathematical skills your child will learn this year—addition and subtraction with regrouping (borrowing and carrying), skip-counting, and multiplication and division readiness, to name a few—will require a solid understanding of numbers and how they work, or number sense. By the end of second grade, your child should have the flexibility to group a set of counters in at least two different ways. If you think your second grader could use more practice in this area, see Number Sense, page 123.

Question 2

Although most second graders can count beyond 100 with little difficulty, many still have little sense of what a certain number means: What does a thousand of something look like? Does it look different from one hundred? By the end of second grade, your child should be able to answer all three of the questions given here. You must, however, be careful in judging your child's answers. If your child guesses the wrong answer, ask him or her about the reasoning behind the guess. For example, your child might guess 100 for the number of leaves on a tree. When you ask, "Why 100?" your child might respond, "Because I looked at that little tree growing out of the sidewalk and it seemed like a hundred." This child has perfectly good reasoning behind his or her estimation. If, on the other hand, your child responds, "Because it seems like a lot," you may want to provide some additional experiences in developing number sense. See Number Sense, page 123, for some suggestions.

Question 3

By the end of second grade, your child will be expected to count and order numbers to 1,000 and to use ordinal numbers appropriately. Notice the numbers that your child missed, if any. For example, if he or she missed 839 and 840 but not 49 and 50, you will want to use numbers in the hundreds to give your child informal practice in ordering numbers. For activity ideas, see Number Sense, page 123.

Questions 4–5

The ability to skip-count and to recognize odd and even numbers shows an understanding of number patterns and helps build a foundation for multiplication and division concepts. By the end of second grade your child should be able to identify odd and even numbers and to skip-count by twos, fives, and tens to 100 and by threes to 30. If you feel your child could use more practice in this area, see Number Sense, page 123, and Multiplication and Division Readiness, page 165.

Questions 6–7

In question 6, your child should be able to pick out the representations of the number twenty-four in boxes a and c. If your child did not pick out *both* correct representations, you may wish to provide some additional support in place value.

By the end of second grade, your child should be able to circle five counters to show what the 5 in 15 means, and ten counters to show what the 1 means. Question 7 asks your child to show what *both* the 5 and the 1 mean. If your child has trouble with this, he or she needs more experience with place value.

Place value is a very difficult concept for most second graders, but it is vitally important to your child's success in mathematics. If you think that your child's understanding of place value could use some strengthening, see Place Value, page 127.

Questions 8–9

These questions evaluate your child's ability to make reasonable estimates. Estimation is an extremely useful skill. Much of the mathematics we use on a daily basis is based on estimation.

In question 8, your child's estimate should have been between 3 and 8. If your child's guess was borderline—3, 8, or 9—you may want to draw a new circle on a sheet of paper and repeat the activity. If the circle holds fewer than 10 pennies, your child's estimate should be no more than three pennies off.

In question 9 your child's estimate should have been within two strides of the actual number of strides. Again, if your child's estimate was borderline—say, within three strides—you may want to repeat the activity using a different distance.

Estimation is a difficult skill that improves only with practice. Practicing estimation will strengthen your child's number sense, problem-solving ability, and computation skill. To reinforce this skill, see Estimation, page 130.

Questions 10–11

Your child will probably spend a great deal of time this year practicing addition and subtraction facts. A quick and accurate knowledge of these facts will give your child a leg up on problem-solving and computation of larger numbers.

Look at the problems that you either circled or checked. Note if the errors fall into any of these categories:

Addition facts through 10: problems a, f, g

Addition facts through 18: problems b, c, d, e, h

Subtraction facts through 10: problems a, b, g

Subtraction facts through 18: problems c, d, e, f, h

At the beginning of the school year, most second grade teachers expect their students to know at least some of their addition and subtraction facts through 10 within five seconds. By the end of second grade, your child will be expected to have a firm grasp on addition and subtraction facts through 18. Look at the answers you circled or checked in the addition or subtraction section.

If you circled more than two problems in a section, your child may be a little shaky with basic addition and subtraction concepts. See Addition and Subtraction Facts Through 18, page 133, and Number Sense, page 123.

If you checked more than two problems in a section, consider the promptness of the response. If your child gave accurate answers but not within the five-second limit, he or she probably uses strategies such as counting up from one number or counting on fingers to arrive at the answers. These strategies are an important, natural step in the process of learning to add and subtract and serve as a bridge to the ultimate goal of automatic response. The more opportunities your child has to practice addition and subtraction facts in fun and varied circumstances, the sooner he or she will be able to recall the answers quickly and accurately. See Addition and Subtraction Facts Through 18, page 133.

If your child answered all the problems correctly within five seconds, he or she already has a fairly sound foundation of math facts. Providing opportunities to use these facts in games and problem-solving activities will strengthen this important foundation. For activity ideas, see Addition and Subtraction Facts Through 18, page 133, and Math Enrichment Activities, page 168.

Questions 12–13

Addition and subtraction of two- and three-digit numbers is traditionally taught at the end of second grade. At that time, most children have little difficulty adding and subtracting numbers that do not require regrouping, but many still struggle with the concept of regrouping. Check to see if your child's errors fall into any of these categories:

Addition with no regrouping required: a, b
Addition with regrouping: c, d
Subtraction with no regrouping: a, b
Subtraction with regrouping: c, d

If your child had difficulty with problems a and b in either the addition or the subtraction section, do not attempt to teach your child addition or subtraction with regrouping (borrowing or carrying) at this time. Instead, give him or her as much support as possible in Number Sense, page 123; Place Value, page 127; and Addition and Subtraction Facts Through 18, page 133. If your child had difficulty with problems c and d in either the addition or subtraction section, you can help by providing experiences in Place Value, page 127, and Adding and Subtracting Larger Numbers, page 143.

Question 14

This question evaluates your child's ability to understand and work with coin values. By the end of the second grade, your child should understand coin values well enough to be able to find two different ways to show the appropriate amounts. If your child was able to show each amount in one way, he or she probably has a good understanding of coin values but needs more experience in order to become more flexible in working with money. To strengthen your child's money sense, see Money, page 149.

Questions 15–16

These questions ask your child to solve money-related problems. By the end of the year most children will be able to give an accurate answer to each of the problems. If your child made an error, think about his or her answer carefully. Was the error a computation error? Or did your child have difficulty figuring out what to do to solve the problem? For additional support in understanding or computing with money, see Money, page 149. For additional support in problem solving, see Problem-Solving, page 162.

Question 17

Many second graders are comfortable with telling time to the hour, half hour, and quarter hour, but still struggle with five-minute intervals such as 10:55 or 9:05. By the end of second grade, most teachers expect their students to be able to read an analog clock to within five minutes. If you'd like to give your child more practice in telling time, see Time, page 152.

Question 18

To be able to solve problems involving time, your child must first have a good understanding of elapsed time—that is, how much time has passed. By the end of the year your second grader should be able to answer correctly each of the questions posed here. A sense of time and its passage is an important life skill. To give your child additional experience in this area, see Time, page 152.

Questions 19–20

This year your second grader will probably practice measuring length, mass, and capacity in both nonconventional units (counters, strides) and standard units (inches, centimeters). By midyear your child should be able to measure the carrot to the nearest counter and inch. To provide more practice in this skill, see Measurement, page 154.

Question 21

Most second graders have had lots of experience with fractions when sharing food or possessions with others. However, it is not uncommon to hear a child say, "Your half is bigger than mine." By the beginning of second grade your child should be able to pick out the picture that shows one-half (the first picture only). If your child had difficulty recognizing that a fraction tells about equal parts, see Fractions, page 156.

Question 22

This question evaluates whether or not your child understands the concept and vocabulary of fractions. By the end of second grade your child should be able to name the shaded part of all three pictures. If your child could name a and b but not c, he or she is probably more familiar with fractions as part of a region (say, dividing up a pizza) than as part of a set (dividing up a bag of apples). An intuitive understanding of both kinds of fractions is critical to future work with fractions. To provide your child with more experience in fraction concepts, see Fractions, page 156.

Question 23

Be aware that the size of the fractional parts in your child's drawing is bound to be approximate. You might need to ask questions such as "Do you want this part to be bigger than that part?" to clarify your child's intentions. Your child's drawing can give you insight into his or her understanding of fractions.

By the end of second grade, your child should be able to draw a picture that shows a close approximation of a fraction (response a). If your child had difficulty performing this task (responses b to e), or if you would like to help strengthen the skills he or she already has, see Fractions, page 156.

Question 24

At the beginning of second grade, most children can identify each of the shapes named here. By midyear your second grader should be familiar enough with the attributes of various shapes to be able to draw them as well. If your child could use more support in this area, see Geometry, page 159.

Question 25

This question explores your child's understanding of the attributes of two- and three-dimensional shapes. Children who have had plenty of experience talking about and manipulating shapes should be able to give correct responses to both questions by the end of second grade. If you feel that your child could use more experience in this area, see Geometry, page 159.

Question 26

Patterns form the basis of our mathematical system, and recognizing patterns is an important problem-solving skill. If your child had difficulty completing this pattern, you may want to provide more experience in recognizing and developing patterns. See Geometry, page 159.

Question 27

This question examines your child's flexibility in thinking about number. Your child should be able to come up with at least *one* number sentence for 7. If your child came up with two or more—especially if both addition and subtraction were included—he or she is well on the way toward gaining the flexibility of thought that is essential to mathematical reasoning. For additional activities that support this ability to think critically, see Number Sense, page 123, and Problem-Solving, page 162.

Questions 28–29

By the end of second grade, your child should be able to solve all of these problems. If your child made an error, think about his or her answer carefully. Was it a computation error? If so, you might want to refer to Addition and Subtraction Facts Through 18, page 133. Or did your child have difficulty figuring out what to do to solve the problem? Notice, too, the strategies your child uses to solve problems. Your child should be comfortable with at least two of the strategies listed. Remember, word problems like these are only one way to evaluate the strategies your child uses to solve problems. You can gain additional insight into your child's problem-solving ability by watching him or her tackle problems that pop up in everyday life. To support and strengthen your child's problem-solving ability, see Problem-Solving, page 162.

Question 30

Grouping and patterning problems like this one show your child's readiness for multiplication and division concepts that will be taught in third and fourth grade. If your child had difficulty supplying either of the missing numbers, or if you would like to give him or her additional experience in this area, see Multiplication and Division Readiness, page 165.

Second grade is a time of consolidating skills and concepts that are vital to your child's future success in mathematics. The more firmly your child grasps these fundamental concepts, the less anxiety your child is likely to feel about math in the future. Even if your child had no difficulty solving the math problems in this assessment, your support and a constant diet of varied math experiences is essential for his or her continuing achievement. Skim through the math exercises in this book and adjust them to fit your child's need. See also Math Enrichment Activities, page 168.

Writing Assessment

Writing skill develops in predictable stages, which are described in detail in Writing Stages and Exercises, page 104. The questions in the Parent Observation Pages will help you look carefully at your child's writing. Compare your findings with the information in Writing Stages and Exercises to determine where your child is in the process of writing. Knowing your child's developmental level will help you respond appropriately to written work and support his or her growth as a writer. Remember, too, that writing and reading skills naturally reinforce each other. By helping your child become a better writer, you will help him or her become a better reader as well.

Reading Exercises

Reading Comprehension

Reading comprehension is measured by questions 3, 6, 9, and 12 on the Reading Assessment.

Pity the poor beginning reader trying to figure out this sentence: "Do fish sleep?" First she must remember to read from left to right, not from right to left, as she does when adding numbers in math. Next, she must know the letters of the alphabet, both uppercase (*D*) and lowercase (all the rest) and have a fairly good idea of the sound each letter stands for. With luck, the young reader will recognize *"Do"* by sight, since the word doesn't follow phonetic rules and can't be sounded out. Still, even to sound out the other words, she needs to know more than simple letter sounds. Let's see, doesn't the letter combination *sh* make a sound all its own? And what was that rule about two vowels that go walking? Oh-oh, what's that squiggly mark at the end of the sentence? Oh, yeah, it's a question mark. Now, what does the whole sentence *mean?*

Learning to read is hard work. Word attack skills like phonics and sight vocabulary are important reading tools, but they are still just a means to an end. Some children can pronounce almost any word you give them, but they have no idea what all those words put together actually mean. Helping your child understand what she has read entails more than asking questions about a reading selection. It means guiding her to focus on meaning even as she is struggling to decode the words. It means teaching her to *think*.

You can help teach your child think while reading in three different ways:

- Model self-questioning during your own reading: "It says here that the president wants 'peace with honor.' Now, I wonder what he means by that."
- Read to your child daily, and ask questions before, after, and as you read aloud to your child or your child reads aloud to you: "Why do you think Ramona's so mad?" "What do you think is going to happen in the next chapter?"
- Play games that reinforce thinking skills your child can use on her own.

Comprehension is thinking, and thinking is harder to teach than the sound of *b* or the sum of 7 + 6. Here are some ways you can reinforce your child's natural ability to think:

- Read to your child daily.
- Help your child read with a purpose.
- Encourage your child to make predictions as she reads.
- Compare and contrast stories, characters, settings, and reactions.
- Talk about causes and effects.
- Help your child use critical reading skills to infer meaning and figure out what's happening.
- Help your child expand her vocabulary.
- Make reading feel special.

Once you are aware of the thinking skills you need to focus on, you will find all sorts of opportunities to reinforce them.

Read to your child daily.

Consider this passage from *Winnie-the-Pooh,* by A. A. Milne:

"Good morning, Eeyore," said Pooh.
"Good morning, Pooh," said Eeyore gloomily. "If it is a good morning," he said. "Which I doubt," said he.

Research has shown that the single largest predictor of a child's long-term success in elementary school reading is the amount of reading aloud that occurs during the child's early years. As a rule, children's listening comprehension is one to three levels higher than their reading comprehension. This means that the stories you read to your child can be more complicated in plot and richer in vocabulary than the books he reads on his own. The conversations you have together while reading give your child a chance to clear up confusing details, check out meanings of words he doesn't know, and, perhaps most important, relate what's happening in the book to his own life. For more about these conversations, see the discussion of critical thinking skills, page 78.

Many parents feel that reading aloud at bedtime is a sacred tradition. For some parents, it's the only time in the hectic day when they're sure to have one-on-one time with their child. Other parents find that both they and their child are tired and grumpy at the end of the day. The parent of an early riser might choose to combine a read-aloud time with her first cup of coffee. Another parent might find that reading aloud is just the thing to occupy a restless, hungry second grader while dinner is cooking. Remember, read to your child for *enjoyment*. There is no greater motivator to read.

A number of excellent bibliographies for children give detailed descriptions of books suggested for each age level. All are available at most libraries. Here are some particularly helpful book lists:

- *Choosing Books for Kids* by Joanne Oppenheim, Barbara Brenner, and Betty D. Boegehold (Ballantine)
- *The Horn Book Magazine,* a highly respected magazine focusing solely on children's literature, which has been publishing reviews of children's books for more than fifty years
- *The New York Times Parent's Guide to the Best Books for Children* by Eden Ross Lipson (Times Books)
- *The Read-Aloud Handbook* by Jim Trelease (Penguin)
- *Reading Rainbow Guide to Children's Books* by Twila Christensen Liggett (Carol Publishing)

To get you started, here are some read-aloud classics that every second grader should know:

PICTURE BOOKS
- *Buffalo Jump,* by Peter Roop (Rising Moon)
- *The Day of Ahmed's Secret,* by Florence Parry Heide and Judith Heide Gilliland (Mulberry)
- *Georgia Music,* by Helen V. Griffith (Greenwillow)
- *Going Home,* by Eve Bunting (HarperCollins)
- *Good Times on Grandfather Mountain,* by Jacqueline Briggs Martin (Orchard)
- *The Kitchen Knight: A Tale of King Arthur,* by Margaret Hodges (Holiday House)

- *Miss Rumphius,* by Barbara Cooney (Viking)
- *Mrs. Katz and Tush,* by Patricia Polacco (Philomel)
- *Mufaro's Beautiful Daughters,* by John Steptoe (Lothrop)
- *Officer Buckle and Gloria,* by Peggy Rathmann (Putnam)
- *Saving Sweetness,* by Diane Stanley (Putnam)
- *Tatterhood and the Hobgoblins,* by Lauren Mills (Little, Brown)
- *Yoshiko and the Foreigner,* by Mimi Otley Little (Farrar, Straus & Giroux)
- *Verdi,* by Janell Cannon (Harcourt)

CHAPTER BOOKS
- *The Black Stallion,* by Walter Farley (Random House)
- *Charlotte's Web,* by E. B. White (HarperCollins)
- *The Chronicles of Narnia,* by C. S. Lewis (HarperCollins)
- *Homer Price,* by Robert McCloskey (Puffin)
- *The Indian in the Cupboard,* by Lynne Reid Banks (Avon)
- *James and the Giant Peach,* by Roald Dahl (Puffin)
- *Just So Stories,* by Rudyard Kipling (Puffin)
- The Little House series, by Laura Ingalls Wilder (HarperCollins)
- *The Lucky Stone* and other books, by Lucille Clifton (Delacorte)
- *My Father's Dragon,* by Ruth Stiles Gannett (Knopf)
- *Ramona the Pest* and other books, by Beverly Cleary (Morrow)
- *Where the Sidewalk Ends* by Shel Silverstein (Harper)
- *The Wind in the Willows* by Kenneth Grahame (St. Martin's)

Help your child read with a purpose.

Although some children delight in deciphering print, most do not get real joy out of reading until it becomes truly useful to them. The horse fancier who can tell you the difference between an Appaloosa and an Andalusian, the computer fanatic who has discovered that a certain software is on sale at Comp-World, the worried student who looks over your shoulder as you write a note to the teacher—all these people have very good reasons for wanting to know how to read. One of the best ways to get your child to *want* to read is to put her in a position where she *needs* to read.

HAVE FIVE MINUTES?

➤ Look it up. What is a light year? Why is April 1 called April Fool's Day? What's the difference between a crocodile and an alligator? Answering your child's difficult questions may be good for your ego, but *not* answering them is better for your second grader's reading skills. Scratch your head, look perplexed, and say, "Hmm, I wonder where we can find the answer." Keep a list of questions on the door of the refrigerator. Then go to the library, use the Internet, or check out reference books you have at home.

➤ No matter what encyclopedia salespeople tell you, you don't have to spend a fortune to build a perfectly adequate reference library in your home. You can start by scanning library sales, Salvation Army stores, want ads, and yard sales for encyclopedias, dictionaries, and other reference books. Answers to many of your child's questions often can be found even in a thirty-year-old edition of the *World Book Encyclopedia*, the *Encyclopedia Britannica*, or *Collier's*. Paperback copies of current almanacs, such as *Information Please* or the *World Almanac*, are often available at reduced prices. Check your child's school book club or large retail stores.

➤ Subscribe to a daily newspaper and use it as a reference tool. Can you go swimming today? Check the paper. Did the Cardinals win last night? Check the paper. Where is *The Lost World* playing? Check the paper.

➤ Follow your second grader's heart. What really gets your child talking a blue streak? Rocks? Horses? Soccer? The latest Disney or space adventure movie? When you don't think you can stand one more baseball statistic or rehash of a movie plot, it's time to hit the library. Don't be concerned if your child leaves with a stack of Disney spin-offs, an advanced geological survey, or even a pile of board books about baby animals. Remember that a second-grade reader needs to *practice reading*. An avid interest will do more toward that end than all of your urging.

➤ Use the library. The library is a no-risk means of letting your child follow her heart's desire. If she gets those six books on wolves home and then suddenly becomes more interested in the human body, just take the books back and let her choose a new stack. Do not discourage her from choosing books that seem too difficult for her. She may do nothing but look at the pictures in a book about astronomy, but she is still practicing reading skills.

➤ If your child refuses to stray from the Berenstain Bears while you gaze longingly at award-winning picture books, you can negotiate a deal. At the library or bookstore, say, "You choose two books, and I'll choose two books." At bedtime, say, "You read Berenstain Bears to me tonight, and I'll read you my favorite book tomorrow night."

➤ Talk about your own reading. Research shows that your attitude is the single most influential factor affecting your child's literacy. Yet your child's view of your reading habits may be very different from your own. How often does she *see* you reading a book, magazine, or newspaper? Does she ever hear you say, "I'll need to read the directions to figure this out"? When you talk about your workday, do you ever mention how much or what kind of reading you did? Who in your family *knows* that your idea of comfort is a hot bath and a good book? These details are not lost on your child. Rather, they say in very clear terms that reading is fun; it's a way to solve problems; it's a vital part of grown-up life.

➤ Read to have fun. Nothing delights a second grader more than telling a good joke. Read comics, joke books, and silly poetry together. Ask your librarian to direct you to books your second grader will split her sides over.

HAVE MORE TIME?

➤ Choose activities that require reading directions. Ask your child to help you read recipes, game instructions, or craft directions. Write down the directions to your child's friend's house, and ask for help in finding the way. Introduce your child to the telephone book and ask her to help you find the number of her favorite toy store.

➤ Set up a simple treasure hunt. Hide a coin or some other small treasure. Then write a series of clues on slips of paper, each clue leading to the next.

➤ Mail a postcard to your child. Children love to get mail. Imagine your child's delight when she receives a postcard from you with a message that she can read herself!

➤ Give your child a subscription to her own magazine. You may want to choose one of the fine children's magazines listed below. If your child has an enduring passion, you might look into adult special interest magazines such as *Sports Illustrated* or *Cat Fancier*. Take some time to look through the magazine together and talk about interesting articles. Even if she can't read all the words, her keen interest will be a great motivator.
  • *Crayola Kids* Magazine
    800-846-7968
  • *Highlights*
    888-876-3809

- *National Geographic World* Magazine
  800-437-5521
- *Ranger Rick's Nature* Magazine
  800-588-1650
- *Spider*
  800-827-0227
- *Sports Illustrated for Kids*
  800-992-0196

Encourage your child to make predictions as he reads.
To be a good reader, your child needs to cultivate the fine art of guessing—guessing what the next word might be, guessing what the character might do next, guessing how the story might end. But guessing is surprisingly difficult for most second graders, who want more than anything to *get it right.* If you think about making predictions as risk taking, you'll understand why the task is so scary. No one likes to fail, and making the wrong prediction feels like failing. You can help your child become a more confident guesser by giving him practice in making predictions.

HAVE FIVE MINUTES?

➤ Choosing a book to read is an act of prediction: Am I going to like this book? What is it about? Before you and your child begin to read a book, ask, "What do you think this book will be about?" "Why do you think that?"

➤ While standing in the checkout line, ask your child to imagine what story might be inside a magazine on the basis of the illustrations or titles on the cover. Be careful which magazines you pick, though—the actual stories might outdo your child's wildest fantasies!

➤ Making predictions is a great time-passer. Here are just a few of the many ways you can fill those extra minutes with some useful practice in guessing what will happen next:
  - In a restaurant: What will each family member order?
  - In the grocery checkout line: What do you think the person next to you is going to have for dinner tonight? What clues are in his grocery basket?
  - On Saturday morning errands: What will be our next stop? The recycling center? The hardware store? The ice-cream shop?
  - On the highway: How many miles will the next sign say it is to Kansas City?

➤ Books that have a rhyming or repeating pattern are often predictable. The refrains from some of your child's favorite books have probably already entered your family's vernacular: "I do not like them, Sam I am. I do not like green eggs and ham!" Continue to share the fun of predictable books with your child. He may still enjoy supplying missing rhymes or chiming in on a repeating pattern, or he may now prefer to switch roles with you, so that he reads most of the text and you chime in. Here are some books that are appropriate for the second grader:

- *And to Think That I Saw It on Mulberry Street!,* by Dr. Seuss (Vanguard)
- *Bringing the Rain to Kapiti Plain,* by Verna Aardema (Dial)
- *City Street,* by Douglas Florian (Greenwillow)
- *Fortunately,* by Remy Charlip (Macmillan)
- *Leonora O'Grady,* by Lean Komaiko (HarperCollins)
- *Mama Don't Allow,* by Thatcher Hurd (Harper)
- *Pickle Things,* by Marc Brown (Parents Magazine Press)
- *Possum Come A-Knockin,* by Nancy Van Laan (Knopf)
- *Tikki Tikki Tembo,* by Arlene Mosell (Scholastic)
- *What Do You Do with a Kangaroo?,* Mercer Meyer (Scholastic)

These delightful storybooks, while not predictable in the traditional sense, are easy to read and afford great opportunities for prediction:

- *The Adventures of Sparrowboy,* by Brian Pickney (Simon & Schuster)
- *Baby Rattlesnake,* by Te Ata (Children's Book Press)
- *The Enormous Crocodile,* by Roald Dahl (Knopf)
- *Flossie and the Fox,* by Patricia McKissack (Dial)
- *It Could Always Be Worse,* by Margot Zemach (Farrar, Straus & Giroux)
- *Jamaica Louise James,* by Amy Hest (Candlewick)
- *The Lonely Lioness and the Ostrich Chicks,* retold by Verna Aardema (Knopf)
- *She's Wearing a Dead Bird on Her Head,* by Kathryn Lansky (Hyperion)
- *The Song of Mulan,* by Jeanne M. Lee (Front Street)
- *Wilfred Gordon Partridge McDonald,* by Mem Fox (Kane Miller)

➤ Your child is no longer a preschooler, and perhaps you've thought that it's time to put storytelling aside. Think again. Traditional stories such as fairy tales, legends, myths, and Bible stories nearly always follow an easy-to-predict cause-and-effect pattern. Try these:

- Fake memory loss in the middle of a familiar tale: "Doggone it! I forgot! Now what's supposed to happen?"
- Take turns telling a tale. Start with a sentence or two—for example, "Once upon a time there lived a spider named Anansi." Then pass the storytelling role on to your child, who might add, "And he lived in a hole in a big round coconut." Keep passing the story back and forth until you come to a great conclusion.
- Turn your child's current worries into a story: "Once upon a time there were two brave knights who were very best friends. One day . . ." Ask your child to help you come up with a solution to the story's problem.
- Tell a new tale and pause at a critical point: "Uh-oh, what do you think Zeus is going to do now?"

You can't quite remember the plot of one of those old stories? Here are some resources:

- *American Fairy Tales: From Rip Van Winkle to the Rootabaga Stories,* compiled by Neil Philip (Hyperion)
- *The Candlewick Book of Fairy Tales,* by Sarah Hayes (Candlewick)
- *D'Aulaire's Book of Greek Myths,* by Ingri and Edgar Parin d'Aulaire (Doubleday)
- *Earthmaker's Tales: North American Indian Stories About Earth Happenings* by Gretchen Will Mayo (Walker)
- *In the Beginning: Creation Stories from Around the World,* by Virginia Hamilton (HBJ)
- *Stories from the Old Testament,* adapted from the King James Bible (Simon and Schuster)
- *When Birds Could Talk and Bats Could Sing,* by Virginia Hamilton (Blue Sky Press)

Compare and contrast stories, characters, settings, and reactions.

HAVE FIVE MINUTES?

➤As you read with your child, ask questions that lead to comparisons and contrasts:
- Does this story remind you of another story we've recently read? Why?
- How is the Paper Bag Princess different from other princesses?
- Which of the Ramona books do you like best?

- Do you think Templeton the rat is a good guy or a bad guy?
- How else could this story have ended?

➤ Make your child's favorite characters part of your daily life. Ask, "How would the Cat in the Hat go about cleaning up this messy room? What do you think Harriet the Spy would be writing in her notebook right now? If you two don't stop squabbling, I'm going to call Mrs. Piggle-Wiggle for a cure!"

HAVE MORE TIME?

➤ Play Botticelli using characters from your child's favorite books. Pretend you are a character—Curious George, for example. Then ask your child to try to guess who you are by asking yes-or-no questions: "Are you a person?" "No." "Are you an animal?" "Yes." "Do you live on a farm?" "No." "Do you sometimes get into trouble?" "Yes." Your child keeps asking questions until she guesses your identity. Then switch roles and try to guess *her* character.

➤ Suggest that your child draw the setting of a favorite story. She might want to make a map (remember the wonderful map of the Hundred Acre Woods in Winnie-the-Pooh books?). Or she might draw some scenery for a fairy tale, or a travel brochure for *Where the Wild Things Are*. These activities will strengthen her powers of visualization—an important comprehension skill.

➤ Ask your child to help you retell a story from another character's point of view. *The True Story of the Three Little Pigs* by Jon Scieszka (Viking) is the wolf's version of what really happened with those pigs. Try *The Three Billy Goats Gruff* from the troll's point of view or Rumpelstiltskin's take on his straw-spinning deal.

Talk about causes and effects.

HAVE FIVE MINUTES?

➤ Talk about the causes and effects of everyday experience. Ask, "What will happen if you let go of that balloon?" or "I wonder what made that tree grow in that funny shape?" Taken to extremes, talking about effects can be a useful way to drive a point home: "If you don't brush your teeth right now, you'll miss the bus. And if you miss the bus, I'll have to take you to school and I'll be late for work. And if I'm late for work, I'll get fired and we won't have any money. And if we don't have any money, we won't be able to pay our rent and we'll be thrown out into the street and starve to death. So go brush those teeth now!"

➤ Play Before and After. Choose a magazine picture or point out an activity on the street that suggests some previous action: a dripping wet dog, a crying child, a teenager fixing a bicycle tire. Ask your child to imagine what happened just *before* the picture or activity. Perhaps the dog chased a duck into a pond, was just given a bath, or ran through a sprinkler. Or imagine what will happen *after* the event: "Watch out, that dog's going to shake water all over us!"

➤ Invent a Rube Goldberg machine. Remember the game Mousetrap? Turning a crank started a chain of reactions (balls rolling, buckets tipping, people springing off diving boards) that eventually dropped a trap on top of a mouse. Decide with your second grader what you want your machine to do—perhaps make lemonade or wake up Dad. On a piece of scrap paper, such as the back of a place mat, draw the first piece of the machine. Then have your child add a piece. Then you add a third piece, and so on. For example, you might draw the hands of a clock. Your child might add a piece of string that pulls a bell when the hand gets to the 12. You might add a cat that is startled by the bell. . . .

HAVE MORE TIME?

➤ Do simple science experiments with your child. Much of science is based on the observation of cause and effect. Simple chemical reactions like the one that creates a baking-powder volcano thrill your second grader as much as they did you years ago.

BAKING-POWDER VOLCANO

You'll need clay or Play-Doh, baking powder, vinegar, and (for an extra thrill) red food coloring. Have your child mold the clay into a volcano shape with a shallow crater on top. Pour a small pile of baking soda and a few drops of food coloring into the crater. Dribble in vinegar, and watch the foaming lava spew out of the volcano!

➤ Libraries and bookstores are filled with books of science experiments ranging from the very easy to the very difficult. The following books are particularly good for second graders:

- *Bet You Can* and *Bet You Can't: Science Impossibilities to Fool You*, by Vicki Cobb (Harper)
- *Chemically Alive! Experiments That You Can Do at Home*, by Vicki Cobb (Harper)
- *Dr. Zed's Dazzling Book of Science Activities*, by Gordon Penrose (Greey de Pencier)
- *Magic Science Tricks*, by Dinah Moche (Scholastic)
- *Simple Science Experiments* (Hans Jürgen Press, Discovery Toys)

➤ If you are really ambitious, you and your second grader might try making a Rube Goldberg machine from materials you find around the house. If you have a computer, your young inventor may enjoy building automated machines with a delightful software program called Widget Workshop (Maxis).

➤ Cook with your child, and talk about it. What makes popcorn pop? Why do onions make you cry? What will happen if you leave the eggs out of that birthday cake? Cooking is full of cause-and-effect relationships. The following books contain easy recipes for food experiments, like making rock candy crystals and frozen emulsion (ice cream):

- *Cooking Wizardry for Kids*, by Margaret Kenda and Phyllis Williams (Barron's)
- *The Science Chef*, by Joan D'Amico and Karen Eich Drummond (Wiley)
- *Science Experiments You Can Eat*, by Vicki Cobb (Harper)

Help your child use critical reading skills to figure out what's happening.

To many of us, "reading comprehension" means finding the main idea in a paragraph on a reading test. In truth, every time your child recounts the plot of a movie or ends a joke with "Get it?" or describes in impassioned terms exactly how his little brother got hit with his baseball bat, he is practicing basic comprehension skills such as summarizing, sequencing, classifying, and drawing conclusions. These skills, sometimes classified as higher-level thinking skills, constitute the "putting it all together" of reading.

HAVE FIVE MINUTES?

➤ Talk about stories as you read together. Your child is probably already adept at reading and discussing at the same time. Perhaps you have experienced reading sessions like this one where a mom is reading *Misty of Chincoteague* to her second grader.

MOM: "... With long brooms and steaming pails of water, they washed the walls and the ceiling of Phantom's stall—"

SECOND GRADER: Wait! Did they already catch Phantom?

MOM: No, it's not even Pony Penning Day yet, remember?

SECOND GRADER: Then why are they cleaning her stall?

MOM: Why do you think?

SECOND GRADER: To get ready for her in case they do catch her?

MOM: Could be! Let's read on and see. "They scraped inches of sand from the hard-packed floor, dumped it in the woods, and brought in fresh, clean sand. They built a manger—"

SECOND GRADER: *A manger!* Isn't that what Baby Jesus was born in?

At this point, Mom flips ahead a few pages and wonders if they'll ever get through this chapter.

Difficult as it is to be patient at times like these, try to remember that good learning is taking place. By going over the sequence of events, by restating the main idea, by asking questions about vocabulary and drawing conclusions, your child is building important comprehension skills. Help him along by demonstrating self-questioning—"Hmm, I wonder if Phantom will like being kept in a stall"—but avoid the temptation to test him on factual information. What he needs most from you is attention, enthusiasm, and occasional help in clarifying his own ideas about what he is reading.

➤ Let your child read ahead of you and fill you in on what happened in the story. You may already be finding that bedtime reading no longer ends when you leave your child's room at night. Perhaps you left the book at Chapter 4 last night, but tonight your sneaky little reader is somehow already on Chapter 6! "Jumping ahead," with its faint taste of one-upmanship, is one of the great joys of learning to read independently. Though you may complain loudly about missing good parts of the story, never stop your eager beaver from reading ahead. Rather, demand a recap of what you missed—especially if he's managed to finish the book!

➤ Play What's Going on Here? The next time you are in a shopping mall or airport, choose an interesting-looking person or situation nearby. Ask your child, "What's going on here?" "What do you think they're arguing about?" "Where do you think that person is going?" Though this game may seem like random speculation, it's also a great way to help your child collect information and summarize events.

➤ Tell each other about your day. Here are a few ways to break the *"Nothin' happened"* pattern:

- Set up a special time—perhaps at the dinner table or just before going to sleep—to tell each other just one special thing that happened during your day.
- Keep a family calendar. Use a month-at-a-glance calendar to record one item about each family member each day. After dinner or just before bed, ask each person to name one thing for you to write in the day's square. (The procedure should take less than five minutes—no elaborate explanations allowed.) At certain intervals have your second grader read your notations and summarize the great moments of your family's life.
- Make headline news. Take turns recapitulating the day's news in headline form: "Dad Breaks All Waiting-in-Line Records!" "Junior Leads Capture the Flag Team to Victory!"
- As an alternative, list a few of your days' accomplishments (or lack thereof) and have your child provide the headline: "Mom Says to Car Salesman: 'Drop Dead.'"

➤Sort and classify. Classifying—grouping objects or ideas by common attributes—is fundamental to both reading comprehension and mathematical reasoning. Luckily, most second graders are great list-makers and organizers. Allow your child to sort anything he can get his hands on—groceries in the shopping cart, coins from your pocket, junk mail, mittens, laundry. Talk about his classification systems, or sorting rules, and encourage him to think of different ways to sort the same group of objects.

➤The next time you're waiting in line, play this variation of Simon Says. Perform a series of movements—pat your stomach, clap, and touch your nose. Then ask your child to repeat the same series of movements in order. To make the game harder, ask your child to repeat only the second movement or only the first two movements. Then switch roles and see how finely tuned *your* sequencing skills are!

HAVE MORE TIME?

➤Make a "Story of My Life" scrapbook. Nothing is more fascinating to a child than his own life. Go through old photos, artwork, birthday cards, and other mementos and help your child glue or tape them into a large scrapbook in chronological order. Help him add captions, narratives, or chapter heads—Chapter 1: I Am Born—wherever needed and encourage him to continue to add meaningful items in the scrapbook whenever he wants.

➤ Make a story map. If you've ever turned to the family tree in the front of a book to keep track of the characters in an epic novel, you know how helpful a visual representation can be. If your second grader is having trouble keeping track of the information he reads or hears, try a graphic organizer such as a Hand Map. After reading a story, spread out your child's hand, palm up. Touch the thumb and say, "Who was the story about?" Then touch each finger and ask:

    Index finger: "What was the main problem in the story?"
    Middle finger: "When did the story happen?"
    Ring finger: "Where did it happen?"
    Pinky: "How was the problem solved?"

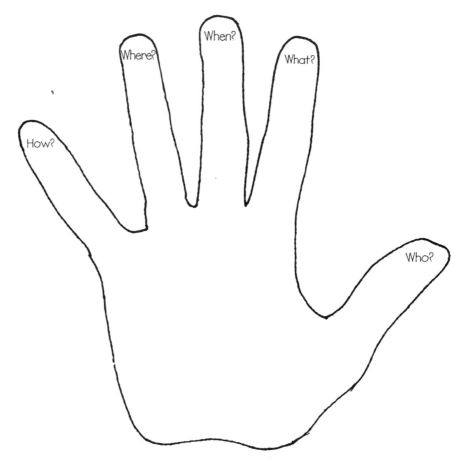

➤ Cut your child's favorite comic strip into separate frames. Scramble the frames, and ask your child to put them back in correct order.

Help your child expand her vocabulary.

HAVE FIVE MINUTES?

➤ As your child's skill in reading increases, so will her joy in discovering new words. Always be on the lookout for interesting words. Keep a small notebook handy so that you can write down wonder words that you come across on errands or in your reading:

"'Pumpernickel?' Wow! What a great word! That's a keeper!"

"'Murophobia?' I don't know what that means. Let's write it down and see if we can find out."

"Do you know whom teddy bears are named after?"

➤ Pass time on car rides by playing the alphabet game. Choose a category, such as animals. The first player names an animal beginning with *a*, for example, "alligator." The next player names an animal beginning with *b*, and so on through the alphabet. Jot down wild guesses (Is there *really* an X-ray fish?) to look up when you get home.

➤ One of the most endearing scenes in children's literature is in E. B. White's *Charlotte's Web*. The ill-tempered rat, Templeton, goes off searching for a word for Charlotte to write about Wilbur the pig. He returns with a word torn from a soap ad: "radiant." Invite your child to use interesting words to describe the people and things in her world. You can serve as a model by stretching your own vocabulary. Don't be afraid to marvel over the *pandemonium* of her *disheveled* room or the *clamor* and *cacophony* coming from the backseat of the car.

HAVE MORE TIME?

➤ Tack up a large sheet of butcher paper or newsprint on your child's bedroom wall. Help her print her favorite words on the sheet. Don't worry if you run out of room or if her current passion switches from palominos to piranhas. Simply tack up another sheet and begin a new list. You might want to suggest that she also add words that keep stumping her in her reading or writing. Take a moment before bedtime to discuss the words' meanings or interesting letter combinations your child might notice. However, avoid the temptation to use these words to drill sight words or to test spelling. Remember, these are your child's special words. How she uses them is up to her.

➤ Play word games. Here are some ways you can satisfy your second grader's love for games and reinforce her vocabulary at the same time:

- Play a simplified version of Fictionary. Choose a difficult word from the dictionary and write down two definitions of it—one correct and one fictional. Your child gets a point every time she chooses the correct definition.
- Adapt commercial word games such as Spill & Spell, Boggle, and Scrabble to reinforce vocabulary by requiring that each word be defined or used in a sentence before it can be counted. One word of caution: many second graders are sticklers for rules, so ask permission before tampering with rules that she may think are set in stone.
- While waiting for food in a restaurant, play a quick variation of Pictionary. Take turns thinking of a word and drawing a picture of it. The opponent must guess the word to get a point. See how many points you can rack up before your food comes.

➤ Don't shy away from classical literature because of the vocabulary. At this point there is probably a big gap between your child's reading comprehension and her listening comprehension. Listening to new words is a lot more comfortable than meeting them on the printed page, and she is still practicing vocabulary skills. If there are words in *Alice in Wonderland* or *Peter Pan* that give you pause, take a minute to figure them out. You will be demonstrating excellent use of context clues. Don't automatically turn to the Disney version of *Winnie-the-Pooh* because A. A. Milne's sentences are so long. The ebb and flow of the language is what wraps such books around your listener's heart. If you feel intimidated by the names in *D'Aulaire's Book of Greek Myths* or by the dialect in Julius Lester's *Black Folktales*, preview the tale before reading it and figure out how you're going to pronounce the words. In the end, your child doesn't really care how you pronounce them; she just wants to hear the story.

Make reading feel special.

Reading is knowledge. Reading is imagination. Reading is adventure. Welcome your child's newfound knowledge into his—and your—life by taking part in and extending the reading experience.

HAVE FIVE MINUTES?

➤Remember to keep reading aloud!

➤Create a special reading nook. Arrange bookshelves to close off a corner of a bedroom, scan yard sales for a special chair (beanbag chairs are particularly popular with the five- to nine-year-old crowd), or set up a small tent in the playroom. If you are really short of space, use a flashlight under the bedcovers or pile up pillows in the bathtub.

➤Invite your reader to tell (or write) his own stories. Suggest that he make up his own *Just So* story or a new adventure for Pippi Longstocking. If he hates the ending of *The Polar Express*, suggest that he come up with a new one. Read the traditional *Little Red Riding Hood* or *Lon Po Po: A Red Riding Hood Story from China* by Ed Young or David Vozar's rap version, *Yo, Hungry Wolf!* Then imagine together what the story would be like if the wolf were a vegetarian or if your child were Red Riding Hood.

HAVE MORE TIME?

➤Some stories lend themselves quite well to an informal readers' theater. Choose parts, including that of the narrator, and read the story aloud as if it were a play, eliminating "he said" and "she said." A note of caution: your second grader may be so taken with the results that he'll want to mount a full-scale production!

➤Help your child write a fan letter to a favorite writer. Write the author in care of the publisher. Most children's publishers—and some authors themselves—respond to their junior fans, even if it is just with a form postcard. Most publishers and many authors also have sites on the Internet and encourage E-mail from young readers.

➤Invite your budding Picasso to respond to a book through art. You'll be surprised how many books lend themselves to art projects. Suggest making a Lost Dog poster for *Henry and Mudge* or a costume like that of the strange creature in *Monkey Monkey's Trick*. Encourage your child to try his hand at an illustrator's style like that of Lois Ehlert, or he might use Eric Carle's collage technique as his model.

Phonics

The ability to use phonics is measured by questions 1, 2, 4, 5, 7, 8, 10, and 11 on the Reading Assessment.

Taught in isolation, phonics rules can be confusing if not downright inconsistent. For example, what is the sound of *s* in these words: *safe, rose, sure?* On the other hand, a few basic rules of phonics taught in the context of enjoyable literature might help your child break the code and get on with the business of enjoying a good read.

Here are five ways you can help your child gain confidence in approaching new words.

1. Encourage your child to write.
2. Review consonant sounds, especially blends (such as *bl*, *str*, and *nd*) and digraphs (such as *ch*, *sh*, and *th*).
3. Practice distinguishing among the short vowel sounds.
4. Review long vowel spellings.
5. Teach diphthongs (such as *aw* in *draw* or *oo* in *boot*) and *r-* controlled vowels (such as *ar* in *car* or *ore* in *store*).

Encourage your child to write often.

Strange as it seems, the path to becoming a good reader is often through writing—and vice versa. Every time your child writes a shopping list, a thank-you note, or an E-mail message to a pal, she is studying words and their phonemic elements. Most second graders have been using their own spelling for a couple of years now. (See the discussion of temporary spelling, page 106.) However, a second grader's natural perfectionism—some teachers call this the year of the eraser—combined with the introduction of formal spelling programs in many schools means that your reader will be looking at words with a new eye.

HAVE FIVE MINUTES?

➤ When your child asks, "How do you spell 'chin'?" do not automatically give her the spelling. Instead, say the word slowly and ask, "What sounds do you hear?" Your second grader might be able to spell the word just by slowing down and listening to the sounds. If she is still stumped, provide help by giving her some examples, as in this typical conversation between a struggling writer and her parent:

"Dad, how do you spell 'chin'?"
"What sounds do you hear?"
"Well, I hear *ch*."
"Yep, *ch* as in your brother's name, Charlie."
"Oh, *ch*!"
"That's right. What else do you hear?"
"'Chin.' I hear an *n*."
"Yep. Now what's in the middle?"
"*E*? No wait, *a*?"
"Listen carefully. Chin—*i*, as in *igloo*."
"Oh, it's an *i*!"
"Right."

➤ Key words, such as *"igloo"* for *i,* reinforce the sound-letter association and can serve as a powerful memory aid for the writer who needs a helping hand. Try these key words for the short vowels or help your child come up with her own: *a*pple, *e*cho, *i*gloo, *o*ctopus, and *u*mbrella.

➤ Take advantage of your second grader's love of codes and secrets. Spell or write out important words in your conversation and encourage her to do the same: "Do we have any *c-a-k-e* left for dessert?"

HAVE MORE TIME?

➤ Many first and second graders keep word files or word books at school to help them gain independence in spelling. Help your child create a word book or personal dictionary to keep at home. Use index tabs to divide a spiral notebook into alphabetical sections. Then ask your child what words she would like to keep in her book. They may be words that she frequently uses in her writing, like "dear" and "birthday," or names, like "Grandma" and "Monroe Street," or just plain interesting words like "electricity" and "avocado." As you help her write the words, discuss sound combinations. For instance, when writing "birthday," you might point out the *ir* combination, the *th* digraph, or the *ay* sound at the end of the word.

➤ Keep a family notebook. Place a spiral notebook in a common area, perhaps by the telephone. Encourage family members to write messages for each other, chore reminders, notes of congratulations or encouragement, and plans for the day in this notebook.

   Help your child read other people's writing and decipher the spelling, but do not correct your child's grammar and punctuation. If you truly get into the habit of using a notebook for your family communication, each entry will serve as a wonderful record of a moment in your family's life.

For more ways to kindle the writing spark, see Writing Stages and Exercises, page 104.

Review consonant sounds, especially blends and digraphs.

HAVE FIVE MINUTES?

➤ If your child asks for the spelling of a word with a blend or digraph in it, give him another word you think he knows with the same digraph in it. "How do you spell 'shark'?"

"It starts with the *sh* sound, just like 'ship.' Do you know what two letters
make the *sh* sound in 'ship'?"

"*Oh!* It's *sh*."

If your child does not pick up the clue, don't force it. Give him the
spelling and let him get on with his writing.

➤ Try this treasure hunt the next time you are waiting for your meal in a
restaurant. Give your child a menu and say, "I'm looking for a word that
begins with the first sound in 'Texas' and ends with the first sound in
'Ohio.' What is it?" If your child finds "taco," he gets to give a hint for you.

➤ As part of their new-found status as elementary school vets, second
graders love to show off their knowledge of playground chants. Little do
they suspect that some of these chants give them much-needed practice in
letter sounds and auditory memory. You can adapt classic alphabet chants
to practice any consonant sounds your child is having trouble with.

The traditional version of one chant goes like this; "*A*, my name is
Alice. I come from Antarctica, and I sell artichokes."

You might give your child a consonant blend—*br*, for example—and
show him how to vary the chant, like this: "*Br*, my name is Bruce, I come
from Brazil, and I sell brontosauruses."

➤ Got some time between innings at a baseball game? Give your child a
program and a pencil and have him circle all the players' names that contain a given consonant sound. In the car, use a map and have him do the
same with place names. This activity also works well with restaurant
menus, cereal boxes, and even—if you *really* need to kill some time—telephone listings!

HAVE MORE TIME?

➤ Do you need to get a certain second grader out from under your feet?
Send him on a scavenger hunt! Make a list of your child's "stickler" consonant sounds. They may be consonants that are easily confused like *b*, *d*,
and *p*; or digraphs such as *th*, *sh*, and *ch*. Give your child the list and send
him off to find objects around the house that begin with the letter sounds
listed. Check his discoveries by having him give each object's name and
location or by accompanying him on a house tour with the consonant list
in hand.

➤ Play hopscotch. Draw a hopscotch pattern on the pavement, but instead
of numbers, write consonants, blends, or digraphs. Players can toss

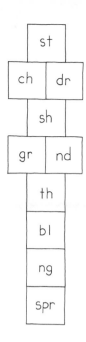

stones or other markers into squares and hop according to hopscotch rules—with one exception. Before hopping, the player must say a word that contains the consonant sound given in the square where his marker has landed.

Is it a rainy day? Use masking tape to make the hopscotch pattern on the living room floor and let your child hop off some of that pent-up energy!

➤ Use an egg carton or muffin tin to play Toss. Print a consonant, blend, or digraph in each cup of the egg carton or on a slip of paper to place in each muffin cup. Place the carton or tin on the floor and take turns flipping a coin into a cup. Say a word that contains the consonant on which the coin lands.

Practice distinguishing among the short vowel sounds.

Second grade is the year of the vowel. Many children still need help with the tricky business of distinguishing among the short vowel sounds (*a* as in *cat*, *e* as in *bed*, *i* as in *sit*, *o* as in *hot*, and *u* as in *cup*). Here are some ways to practice.

HAVE FIVE MINUTES?

➤ As you read with your child, notice if she has difficulty distinguishing between short vowel sounds—confusing "cat" with "cot," for example. Use key words to help her remember the sound: "Look at the word 'cot.' It has an *o* in it, like 'octopus.'"

➤ It's exciting to a child to catch a parent's mistake. As you read aloud school notices, highway signs, or game directions, make a point of occasionally misreading a word that has a short vowel sound: "Come to Shop 'n' Save this weekend for bug savings." If your child doesn't catch the mistake, you might try muttering, "Bug savings? No, wait a minute. That doesn't seem right."

➤ Play Pass the Word. Start with a short-vowel word such as "bed." Have your child change the *e* to a different vowel to make a new word, such as "bad." Then you change the vowel again to make yet another word—for example, "bid." Take turns until you run out of short vowels that make words. Then begin again with a new word.

HAVE MORE TIME?

➤ Make a short-vowel flip book. Fold three sheets of paper vertically in half and staple them along the fold. Make two long cuts to divide the book into three sections, as shown. Write the letters *b, d, h, s, l, r* on the left-hand pages; *a, e, i, o, u* on the middle pages; and *g, t, n, d, p, m* on the right-hand pages. Help your child flip the pages to make as many different words as possible.

➤ Use chalk to draw three circles on the pavement. Inside the first circle, write the letters *b, d, h, r,* and *sh.* In the second circle, write *a, e, i, o, u.* And in the third circle, write *d, g, ll, n, p.* The object of the game is to make as many words as possible by choosing one letter or letter pair from each circle. Begin by tossing a stone into the first circle, choosing a letter or letter pair, and writing it on the pavement. Do the same for the second and third circles, adding those letters to the first to make a complete word. Take turns with your child to see how many words you can make using various combinations from the circles.

Unfortunately, the English language does not always follow its own phonetic rules. Think about the vowel sound in the words "bed," "head," and "said." If your child makes a nonexistent word such as "hed," congratulate him on his choice of sounds, give him the correct spelling, and tell him you will save tricky words like "head" for another game.

For an indoor version of this game, draw the circles on the back of a place mat while waiting for your food in a restaurant. Take turns flipping pennies into the circles.

➤ Choose a fun word with lots of vowels in it, like *"hippopotamus."* Ask your child how many three-letter words he can make from the letters in *"hippopotamus"*—for example, *"hip," "hot," "pot," "sat."* For an extra challenge, try using four-letter (*ship, math*) or five-letter (*stump, thump*) words.

Review long vowel spellings.

The good news here is that long vowel sounds (*a* as in *cake, e* as in *Pete, i* as in *kite, o* as in *home,* and *u* as in *cube*) are a lot easier to hear than short vowel sounds. Unfortunately, what is easy to hear is not always so easy to spell. Think about how the *i* sound is spelled in these words: *hide, find, die, might,* and *fly.*

Luckily, you can clear up some of the confusion by making sure your child knows two simple rules:

1. A silent *e* makes the vowel say its name, as in *cave, Pete, hide, stove,* and *rude.*
2. When two vowels go walking, the first one does the talking. When two vowels are together in a word, the first vowel is long and the second vowel is silent, as in *rain, bead, lie, goat,* and *glue.* The exceptions to this rule are often vowel combinations beginning with *o* (*oi, ou, oy*).

HAVE FIVE MINUTES?

➤ Point out the magic *e.* As you read with your second grader, point out words with silent *e.* Say, "This word has a magic *e.* What does the vowel say?" Ask your child to find magic *e* words on signs, in headlines, or in advertisements.

➤ When you're reading aloud to your child and you come to a word with a vowel digraph (*ea, oa, ue*), cover the second vowel with your finger and say, "That second vowel made this one say its name. What is it?"

HAVE MORE TIME?

➤ Tell your child that you are going to perform a magic trick. On the left side of an index card, print a word that can be changed by adding a silent *e* to the end—*cut, not, past,* or *spin,* for example. Fold over the right side of the card to create a flap, and print the letter *e* on the flap, as shown. Unfold the flap and ask your child to read the first word. Then fold over the flap and, *voilà,* a new word appears! Use the list below for other magic *e* words, or follow your child's suggestions:

cap (cape)   grip (gripe)   hat (hate)
dim (dime)   plan (plane)   rip (ripe)
rod (rode)   spin (spine)   tap (tape)

➤ Make a word wheel. Cut two circles from poster board, one larger than the other. Print the following long-vowel spellings around the edge of the large circle: *ain, ake, eat, ice, oat, ute.* Then print these consonants along the edge of the smaller circle: *c, b, m, ch, fl, st.* Use a brass fastener to attach the smaller circle to the larger circle. Help your child spin the wheel and decide if the combined letters make a word.

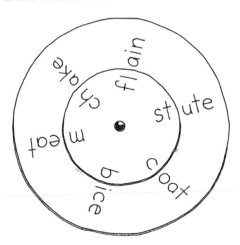

Teach your child vowel diphthongs.

Diphthongs (such as *aw* in *draw* or *oo* in *boot*) and *r*-controlled vowels (such as *ar* in *car* or *or* in *store*) are especially tough because they have neither the long nor the short vowel sound. The more practice children have reading words with these vowel sounds, the easier they are to recognize.

Diphthongs	*r-controlled Vowels*
oy (boy), oi (boil)	ar (star)
ow (how), ou (ouch)	er (sister)
oo (book), oo (spoon)	ir (first)
ew (dew)	or (north)
au (sauce), aw (lawn), all (ball)	ur (turn)

HAVE FIVE MINUTES?

➤ In your reading and in your speech, occasionally point out the sound and spelling of *er* at the end of a word, as in *flower, mother, after, over.* See how many words you and your child can think of that end with *er.*

➤ When your child comes to a word with a diphthong or *r*-controlled vowel while reading, frame the letters with your fingers. Ask her to recall the sound that the two letters make. If necessary, give her a prompt: "*o-y,* as in 'toy.'"

➤ Diphthongs are hard. The same sounds are spelled differently (sauce, lawn, all), and the same spellings *sound* different (book, moon). As you read with your child, occasionally point out the diphthongs in words. Have your child find other words with either the same sound or the same spelling. Talk about the similarities and differences in sounds and spellings.

➤ Label three columns *oy, all, er,* or other vowel combinations your child needs practice recognizing. Help your child write down as many words containing those vowel combinations as you can think of. Then see how many words you can use in a story that you make up together.

HAVE MORE TIME?

➤ If your child is having trouble reading words containing *r*-controlled vowels, try this classic spelling activity. Write the following words across the top of a sheet of paper, and have your child read them aloud: cat, he, chip, spot, bun. Then say, "I know a little rascal named *r* who wants to play mischief with these words. Look what happens to cat when that rascal *r* slips in!" Write "cart" under "cat" and help your child read the word. Then ask your child to show and tell you what the rascal *r* does to the rest of the words in the list.

➤ Play rhyming Four Square. Mark off four squares on the pavement. Each player stands in one square. The first player says a word, like *"down,"* and bounces the ball to another player. The player who catches the ball says a word that rhymes with *"down"* and bounces the ball to another player or back to the first player. Play continues until you run out of rhymes or a player misses the ball. Then play resumes with a new starter word. Do not be concerned if the rhyming words have different spellings as in *"dirt"* and *"hurt."* The object of this game is to work on hearing the vowel sounds.

Word Study

The ability to recognize word parts is measured by questions 1, 2, 4, 5, 7, 8, 10, and 11 on the assessment.

The process of sounding out words can be painfully slow, even for readers who are comfortable with making letter-sound connections. To become a fluent reader, the second grader must develop shortcuts to unlocking the meaning behind the printed word. Learning to recognize common word parts is one such shortcut.

Word study is really nothing more than wordplay: taking words apart and putting them back together again. Here are four kinds of wordplay that will help your child become a more fluent reader.

1. Practice hearing syllables in words.
2. Practice recognizing base words and compound words.
3. Teach these word endings and their meanings: *s, es, ed, ing, er, est.*
4. Practice recognizing contractions: *isn't, I'll, we've, she's, they're.*

Practice hearing syllables in words.

Quick! What's this word: *triskaidekaphobia?* If your eyes crossed at the mere length of the word, then you know how many second graders feel when they come across a word consisting of more than five letters. Breaking words into smaller parts makes the task more manageable. (By the way, *triskaidekaphobia* is the fear of the number 13.)

➤ When you are reading aloud and you come across an unfamiliar name or long word—*remember,* for example—show your child how to break the word into syllables to figure it out. Put your finger over all but the first syllable and read that syllable: *re.* Then move your fingers so that only the first two syllables show, and read the two syllables together: *re-mem.* Continue until you've sounded out the entire word.

➤ If your child stumbles over a long word while reading aloud to you, do *not* insist that he sound out each syllable in the word. This may serve only to bog him down and make him lose track of the meaning of what he is reading. However, you might try covering all but the first syllable of the word. If your child is reading for meaning, he may need only the first syllable to figure out the word.

➤ Clap, stamp, or snap out the syllables of your name, your dog's name, or any other interesting word. Then count the claps: *Rob-in-son*—three syllables. Challenge your second grader to think of words with even more syllables.

➤ Choose a word that is easily divided into two syllables—for example, *notebook.* Use a body movement such as a jumping jack to emphasize the two word parts: hands above your head, feet out for *note;* hands at your sides, feet together for *book.* Encourage your child to make up his own body movements for words with two, three, and four syllables. Repeating patterns of movement can help children develop new memory pathways.

HAVE MORE TIME?

➤ Play Toss-Up by tossing a ball against a garage door or a cement wall and letting your child catch it on the rebound. Then have him toss the ball for you to catch. Now call out a word as you toss the ball. Your child must count the number of syllables in the word and let the ball bounce that number of times before catching it. Take turns calling out words and catching the bouncing ball.

➤ Go on a syllable scavenger hunt. Ask your child, "How many four-syllable words can we think of in four days?" Write your child's estimate at the top of a sheet of paper and attach it to your refrigerator. Whenever you and your child come across a four-syllable word—*refrigerate!*—write it on the sheet. At the end of four days, see how close you came to your estimate.

Practice recognizing base words, also known as roots, and compound words.

Recognizing the little words inside big words can make a frighteningly long word, like *notwithstanding*, approachable. Be aware, however, that this technique doesn't always work. Splitting *breakfast* into *break* and *fast,* for example, might do more harm than good!

HAVE FIVE MINUTES?

➤ If your child gets stuck on a word that has a familiar base, or root, cover everything but the base and have her read only that part of the word. She may be able to figure out the word's meaning just by knowing its base word.

➤ Tell your child that many words, like many people, live in families. The words in word families are similar in some way, just like the people in families are often similar in some way. Choose a word such as *play*, and see how many other words you and your child can think of that belong to the same family: *plays, played, player, playing, playful, playground, playmate, playpen.*

➤ Give your child the excitement of catching you in a mistake as you read aloud. When you come to a word that has a familiar base, such as *helpful,* change the base to another—for example, *handful.* Let your child correct you by pointing out the difference in the two base words.

➤ Take advantage of your second grader's love of riddles. Riddles often make use of the literal meanings of compound words. Even the following old standbys may be delightfully new to your second grader. Try them. Then see if, together, you can come up with more of your own:
What do you call a dog that can tell time? (A watchdog.)
What do you call sleepy cattle? (Bulldozers.)
What does a spider spread on her toast in the morning? (Butterflies.)

HAVE MORE TIME?

➤ Have you ever seen a house fly or a fish bowl? Compound words can be great fun to illustrate, especially when the parts don't necessarily add up to the whole. Brainstorm a list of compound words with your child, or use the list below. Suggest that your child choose a word and illustrate its literal meaning. Then see if you can guess the word.

ballroom	bulldozer	butterfly
carpool	cupcake	grasshopper
pigtail	rainbow	

➤ At a restaurant, write the following parts of compound words on a napkin or on the back of a paper place mat. Challenge your child to write down as many compound words as he can using different combinations of the word parts. See how long a list he can come up with before the food arrives.

any	where	fire
some	one	place
day	time	birth

Teach these word endings: s, es, ed, ing, er, est.

Familiar words have a habit of becoming unfamiliar when an ending is added. Children who can recognize common word endings are less likely to be confused by the new ending and more likely to focus on the meaning of the base word.

HAVE FIVE MINUTES?

➤ When your child comes to a word with one of these endings while reading, frame the ending with your fingers and have him recall what sound the ending makes.

➤ Whenever possible, use the endings *er* and *est* when making comparisons in daily conversation. Just be sure the comparisons are descriptive rather than judgmental: "This clay bowl is a little rounder than your last one," not, "Your pictures are always so much neater than your sister's."

➤ The next time you have a few minutes to spare, try this game of I Spy. Choose an object and then give a hint by comparing it to something else: "I spy with my little eye something that is *wider* than my foot" (the sidewalk). "I spy with my little eye the *youngest* person in this room" (an infant). Try to use the endings *er* and *est* whenever possible, but don't insist upon it. It's the comparisons that count.

➤ To pass time in the waiting room at the doctor's office, fold a sheet of paper into thirds. Print comparative words on each third, for example, *fierce, fiercer, fiercest.* On one third, draw a picture of a fierce-looking animal. Say, "Look, I made a fierce tiger. Can you make one that's even fiercer? Now let's make the fiercest one of all!"

HAVE MORE TIME?

➤ Play Categories with words that have the same endings. Suggest a category, such as "Things I Have in My Toy Box," and a rule such as "The word must name more than one." Then take turns naming items found in the toy box: "In my toy box, I have two broken walkie-talkies, nine Beanie Babies, and 243 Lego blocks." Here are some other possibilities:

Category	Rule
Things I Did as a Baby	The word must end in *ed* (cried, crawled).
Things You Can Do in the Snow	The word must end in *ing* (sledding, skiing).
Jobs	The word must end in *er* (teacher, gardener).
The Most	The word must end in *est* (biggest, meanest).

➤ Magnetic Poetry for Kids is a commercially produced collection of magnetized words and word parts. Place a list of words and a second list of word endings on your refrigerator, a file cabinet, or a cookie sheet. See how many different words you and your child can make from the two lists.

If you wish to make your own magnetic words, look for magnetic sheets in an office supply store. Snip the sheets into word-size strips. Use an indelible marker to write words and endings on the strips.

Practice recognizing contractions.

Most second graders are expected to be familiar with the contractions of *is (it's), are (you're), has (he's), have (we've), will (I'll)* and *not (can't)*. Your child may already recognize many of these as sight words, but understanding their structure and meaning can help him identify new contractions as well.

HAVE FIVE MINUTES?

➤ Take a minute to point out contractions in your reading. Say, "'We've.' Hmm. I'll bet that's a contraction. What two words do you think *we've* stands for?"

➤ If your child asks where to place the apostrophe in a contraction that she is writing, first ask what two words the contraction stands for. Next, ask what letter or letters were left out in the contraction. Remind your second grader that the apostrophe goes in the exact position where the letters once appeared.

➤ Your second grader may also be trying to sort out the difference between a contraction (*"He's* late"), a possessive (*"Fred's* cat"), and a plural ("two *cats"*). This is no mean feat! Some second graders solve the problem by throwing in an apostrophe wherever they think it looks good. (This isn't just a second grade problem. Have you ever seen *"Today's Omelet's,"* or something similar, written on a restaurant chalkboard?) This tendency is a common by-product of learning a new skill. You will probably find that it corrects itself fairly quickly as your second grader becomes more comfortable with the skill. If all those apostrophes still drive you crazy, do try *not* to focus on mistakes in your child's writing. Instead, occasionally point out an interesting word that contains an apostrophe and chat about how the apostrophe is used.

➤ Play Pass the Contraction. Give your child two words, such as *do* and *not* and ask him to give you the contraction (*don't*). See how many contractions you can get through before you reach the front of whatever line you're standing in.

HAVE MORE TIME?

➤ Use magnetic letters, Scrabble tiles, or letters written on squares of paper to give your child a concrete understanding of contractions. Make a large apostrophe out of construction paper. Now use the letters to construct two words, for example, *you* and *will*. Move the words together. Then take away the *w* and the *i* and replace them with the apostrophe. Have your child read the new word. Repeat the activity with two new words. When your child gets used to the pattern, have him create his own contractions.

➤ Chant the words that make up contractions to the tune of the Campbell Soup jingle. Repeat the song using as many words and their contractions as possible.

You are, you're   Is not, isn't.
You are, you're   Is not, isn't.
This is my contraction: This is my contraction:
You are, you're.   Is not, isn't.

Sight Words

The ability to read sight words is measured by questions 1, 2, 4, 5, 7, 8, 10, and 11 on the assessment.

Read this sentence. Now go back and sound out each word in the previous sentence. Imagine how long it would take you to read this book if you had to sound out each word on every page! Chances are that the first time you read that sentence you recognized every word instantly by sight. Most competent adult readers have a sight vocabulary of more than 100,000 words.

For your child to become a fluent reader, she too must build a sight vocabulary that she can count on. Luckily she probably has had a good start. At age two she recognized *Cheerios*. At four, she knew *brontosaurus* and *Tyrannosaurus rex*. *McDonald's, ice cream,* and *Beanie Babies sold here* might now be part of her expanding vocabulary of sight words that she never had to sound out. Though you may wish that your second grader didn't recognize *McDonald's* quite so readily, remember that recognizing and remembering print—*any* print—is a critical part of learning to read. When you respond positively to your child's attempts to make sense of print, you reinforce these all-important attitudes toward reading:

- Reading is useful.
- Reading is fun.
- Reading is something I can share with people I love.
- I can read!

Still, it seems a long way from *McDonald's* to the 3,000 sight words most children have mastered by the end of third grade. How can you possibly help?

Every time you read to your child, every time she reads to you, and every time you spell out "and *y-o-u* spells 'you'!" during a game of tag, you are helping your child learn sight words. Recognition takes practice, and the only way to practice reading is to read. Reading teachers say that it takes more than a hundred *meaningful* exposures to a word to make it part of a reader's sight vocabulary. Although flash cards and other drills might seem to increase the number of exposures your child has to a word, they separate the word from its meaning. When a word is separated from its meaningful context, it loses the powerful association that makes it memorable. How much better it is to help your child build a bank of sight words that she associates with discovery and fun.

Your second grader will need to recognize two different types of sight words: those that do not follow the rules of phonics, such as *what* and *though,* and those that appear frequently. Recognizing the frequently used words is especially important. Although the English language includes nearly half a million words, one-third of all our written material is made of only twenty-two words. And just one hundred words make up one-half of all written material! Here is a list of the fifty most frequently used words.

a	all	an	and	are
as	at	be	but	by
can	do	each	for	from
had	have	he	here	him
how	I	if	in	is
it	not	of	on	one
or	said	she	that	the
there	they	this	to	use
was	we	were	what	when
which	will	with	you	your

HAVE FIVE MINUTES?

➤ Encourage your child to reread her favorite books. These highly predictable books will give her sight vocabulary much needed reinforcement and will bathe her in the grand feeling of competence.

➤ Suggest that your child use the predictable pattern of a favorite story or rhyme to write her own version. This second grader's version of "Old MacDonald" gave her good practice in sight vocabulary as well as a good case of the giggles! The sight words are italicized:
Kayla Larson *had a* bed.
E-i-e-i-o!
And under her bed, *there were* dirty socks.
E-i-e-i-o!

➤ Have something to say? Write it down! Attach a reminder about a chore to the refrigerator. Leave an "I love you" message for her to find on her pillow at night or in her lunchbox at noon. Write down telephone messages, weekend plans, and birthday party ideas, and encourage your child to do the same. Look at how many high-frequency words (set in italics) this seven-year-old used in one very sincere letter of apology to her brother:

Dear Kyle,

I am sorry *I* hit *you*. *It is* just *that I was* mad *and you were the* closest thing *to* hit. Next time *I will* try *to* find something else *to* hit.

Marissa

For more ideas on how to inspire your child to write, see page 104.

HAVE MORE TIME?

➤ Go on a sight-word scavenger hunt. Choose two pages from familiar books or, for a harder version, two paragraphs from the newspaper. Make sure that both pages or paragraphs have about the same number of words in them. Choose a word from the list on page 99 for each of you to find. It can be the same word, or you may choose different words. Use tally marks to record the number of times the chosen word appears in the selection. Then compare tallies to see whose selection had the most occurrences.

➤ Because they often lack content, sight words are more easily learned in context rather than on flash cards. Make a copy of the phrase cards on page 190, or write simple phrases containing one or more frequently used words—the more common the phrase, the better—on index cards. See how many phrases your child can read in a limited period of time. Then make a game of building a sentence or story around each phrase.

If your child likes card games, you can use these cards to play any number of old standards. Make a duplicate set of cards so that you have two cards for every phrase.

- Go Fish. Shuffle both sets of cards together. Deal out five cards for each player and place the rest face down in the "pond." Try to form pairs by asking each other for cards—"Do you have 'she said'?"—and choosing cards from the pond. The player with the most pairs wins.
- Bingo. Use one set of cards. Make bingo boards, as shown, and use pennies as markers. Each board should have the same phrases located in different squares. Place the phrase cards face down and take turns choosing a card and calling out the word. The first player to cover a row vertically, horizontally, or diagonally is the winner.

at the store	go to school	here or there	which one
each one	how are you	what is that	all I have
from him	I love you	you and me	by the way
if I were	she said	come with me	I will do it

how are you	I love you	by the way	each one
what is that	I will do it	she said	come with me
all I have	you and me	if were	from him
which one	here or there	at the store	go to school

each one

- Concentration. Shuffle both sets of cards together. Place the cards face down in rows. Take turns turning over pairs of cards to see if they match. The player with the most matching pairs wins.

- Board games. Adapt a game board that you already own, such as Trivial Pursuit, by reading phrase cards instead of answering questions. Or help your child make a simple game board based on a sport or other current interest. Players roll the die and move a certain number of squares only after reading a phrase card correctly. File folders with pockets make great game boards. You can draw the game on the folder's blank inside surface and use the pocket to store the phrase cards.

Fluency

As a second grade reader, your child is working very hard to decode words automatically, to recognize sight words, to make predictions about what's coming up, and to correct himself whenever he misreads "house" for "horse." Fluency is the end result of all that work. Your second grader has to practice, practice, practice until those skills become second nature and he is free to concentrate on the meaning of what he is reading.

Put simply, the more you read to your child, the better he will read and think. And the more your child reads, the more fluent and natural his reading will become. Here are some things you can do to help him in the process.

HAVE FIVE MINUTES?

➤ Don't confuse fluency with the ability to read aloud. Even gifted readers are sometimes terrible at reading orally, since their minds move far ahead of the words they are actually reading. Think about the last time you were asked to read something aloud at a meeting or at your place of worship. Even if you are a confident reader, chances are you hoped for some rehearsal time. Give your child the same advantage. Before he reads aloud to you, suggest that he take a few minutes to read the selection silently. That bit of preparation will add greatly to your child's oral fluency and confidence.

➤ Use a bookmark. By second grade, many schoolchildren are being urged not to use their fingers to point to their place as they read. While the theory behind this instruction is sound—finger-pointing does make for choppy, word-by-word reading—it ignores the fact that some second graders may still have difficulty tracking words visually. A bookmark will help your child stay on track. At the same time it will encourage him to read line by line rather than word by word.

➤ Do not overcorrect your child. Resist the temptation to make a struggling reader sound out every word. If your child stumbles, suggest that he do what most fluent readers do—guess at the word or skip it and read on. He can come back to the word later when the meaning of the entire sentence becomes clearer.

➤ Encourage your child to reread old favorites. You may think that by now he should have outgrown *Brown Bear, Brown Bear, What Do You See?* and *The Very Hungry Caterpillar.* Yet the comfort and confidence your child feels while reading these books is valuable for developing fluency.

➤ Help your child choose books that are at an appropriate reading level. Librarians sometimes use the five-finger rule when helping children choose a book. Have your child read a page from the book and hold up one finger each time he comes to a word he doesn't know. If by the end of the page, he has five or more fingers held up, the book is too hard for *independent* reading. This doesn't mean it isn't a good selection for shared reading or other uses, though. If your child is interested in the book, by all means read it aloud to him.

HAVE MORE TIME?

➤ Do some "whisper reading." The next time your child reads aloud, ask if you can read along with her. Then do so, but in a very low voice. If she is reading with confidence, you should barely whisper. Where she needs more support, raise your voice slightly. If she stumbles over a word, provide it for her. Read at a slightly faster rate than your child might ordinarily read aloud, but not so fast that she falls behind. You are there to support her, not to race with her!

➤ Although there are lots of early reading series on the market, choosing books for the newly independent reader can be difficult. Many are tired of tried-and-true beginning readers like *The Cat in the Hat*, but haven't quite made the transition to more difficult chapter books. The easy-to-read books listed below might give your second grader some variety while keeping her reading experience successful and fluent.

- *The Case of the Hungry Stranger* and other Private Eye Club books, by Crosby Bonsall (Harper & Row)
- The Commander Toad series, by Jane Yolen (Coward)
- The Dragonling series, by Jackie French Koller (Pocket Books)
- The Marvin Redpost series, by Louis Sachar (Random House)
- The Nate the Great series, by Marjorie Weinman Sharmat (Coward)
- The Old Turtle series about sports, by Leonard Kessler (Dell)
- *The Stories Julian Tells* and *More Stories Julian Tells,* by Ann Cameron (Pantheon)

And just in case you missed some of the children's classics, here are a few favorites:

- The Fox and His Friends series, by Edward Marshall (Dial)
- The Frog and Toad series, by Arnold Lobel (HarperCollins)
- *Green Eggs and Ham* and other books, by Dr. Seuss (Random House)
- The Henry and Mudge series, by Cynthia Rylant (Simon & Schuster)

➤ Let your child read junk. Think of your own reading habits. Aren't there times when all you want is a good old-fashioned page-turner? A little junk never hurt anybody. A child who is just beginning to read independently has a voracious appetite for print. He will get on kicks that drive you crazy. You might find yourself moaning, "Just how many Boxcar Children books *are* there?" But remember that the Boxcar Children books today give your child what a hundred readings of *Where's Spot* gave him a few years ago—comfort, familiarity, predictability, and most of all *practice.* If you don't like the books, tell him why. But unless you find a book truly offensive to your values, go ahead and let him read. Just make sure you continue to provide as many supplements to that diet as you can.

Writing Stages and Exercises

Smoky Quartz is my cat. He is nice and calm. He's cute. Well, I think so. And he looks like a lion when he's resting. And he's gray.

You will need one or more writing samples, as suggested in the Writing Assessment on page 54, to determine your child's current stage of writing development.

Is this scene familiar? Your second grader comes home proudly waving a slightly crumpled sheet of paper and says, "I wrote a story! It's called a bio-something and it's about somebody's life. Mine's about Smoky, and I'm going to send it to Grammy and Gramps 'cause they're the ones who gave us Smoky!"

Impressed that the kid who could barely write her name in kindergarten is now writing full-length biographies, you eagerly take a look:

"Smoky Qartz is my cat. He is nice and com. Hes cute. well I think so. And he looks lik a lion wen hes resting. And he gray."

Your heart drops. You think, "This can't go to Grammy and Gramps. It's a mess!" When it comes to communication, you have probably always been your child's number one fan. From her first "da-da-da-da" to the bright scribbles that still hang on your kitchen wall to the hand-drawn "Get Beeter!" card that makes you smile every time you see it, you have oohed and aahed every step of the way. The process has seemed perfectly easy and natural. No infant was ever as clever, no preschooler ever as perceptive, no first grader ever as artistic. Then came second grade.

Your child has been scribbling, drawing, and writing the letters of the alphabet for years, but writing seems to have gotten *serious* all of a sudden. Somewhere along the line a subtle, or perhaps not so subtle, change in your expectations has occurred.

Think carefully. What is it that you want your child to be able to do? You want her to be able to write. But what does that mean? For most people, being able to write means being able to communicate effectively. It means, above all, not being *afraid* to write. In second grade two statements—"You've got to make sure other people can understand your writing" and "You mustn't be afraid to write"—seem contradictory. How can you help your child succeed at the first goal without jeopardizing the second? Look at these possible responses to the Smoky story above:

"Wow, that's a great story! It really tells a lot about Smoky!" Keep in mind that you are your child's first, most appreciative, and (at least until adolescence) most important audience. If you exclaim delightedly over your child's writing, she will think, "Wow, Mom likes it!" If you offer a specific constructive comment, she will think, "Wow, Dad is really thinking about this, and he really likes it!" If you criticize the mechanics and spelling, your child will think, "Well, he said he liked it, but I guess he didn't really mean it."

"I like where you said he looks like a lion. It really gives me the picture that Smoky is strong and proud." Find one thing that your child has done well and point it out. If your second grader hears that she is doing something well, she will probably try to repeat her success. In fact, if this story is successful, you may even see a series of stories about Smoky.

"You wrote, 'Smoky is gray.' That really helps people imagine what he looks like. Can you see any other colors in his fur?" By asking your child to tell you more, you are laying the groundwork for good revision. This piece may not—and probably should not—be revised. But the next time your child writes a description, you may find that she may observe, and write, a few more details.

"Grammy and Gramps would love this story! Let's make a special copy to send to them." If your child is writing a lot at school, she probably already knows that most good writing isn't a one-shot deal—that it takes a few first drafts to get a piece of writing where you want it to be. As your child copies the story onto her kitty cat stationery or types it into the computer, you can ask if there are any words whose spellings she thinks might need a double-check. Or, if your child has already worked long and hard on this story, you might suggest just one finishing touch—a signature or a small illustration, perhaps, or one last look to see if every sentence ends with a period.

"Wow, you did a really good job figuring out the letters in Quartz. The way we usually spell it has just one more letter. Do you remember what letter comes after *q* in words like 'quit' and 'queen'?" If you feel you must comment on spelling or punctuation, make sure you do so only after you have reacted appreciatively to the meaning, imagination, and spirit in your child's words. Don't correct every mistake in the piece. Instead, choose *one* spelling pattern or rule of mechanics that you think your child might be close to knowing. If your child can already spell "quit," "quack," and "queen," for example, she may be quick to realize that the letter *q* is usually followed by a *u*.

Developmental Stages of Writing

Think back on how your child learned to talk. Even the most precocious children don't just wake up one morning and start to speak in sentences. Learning to talk was a slow process—one that your child is even now refining. Learning to write is a lot like learning to talk. Both skills are born of a burning desire to tell others what you need or what you think. Children naturally want to make themselves understood through writing. A young child scribbles, then begins to form letters, then links the letters with sounds and begins to make words. By second grade, most children are combining words into sentences and beginning to figure out that standard spellings make words easier for other people to read.

All children who are beginning to write generally go through the same stages of learning. In the first stage, children know that writing—especially writing letters of the alphabet—conveys a message. You may still have some samples of this stage of your child's writing—pages full of very important scribbles and random letters.

As your child gains practice and maturity, she moves into another stage: she begins to identify the sounds of consonants and uses those consonants to represent words. This is the stage that looks like those old ads for speed-writing courses: "If u cn rd ths . . ." A child in this stage rarely uses vowels (oddly enough, she may use the letter *r* instead); she can spell some frequently used words like "the" or family names; and she often runs words together or separates them with dots. If your child is in this stage, you might not always be able to read what she writes. Ask her to read her story aloud, and then ask if you may lightly pencil in some of your own spellings so that you both always know what the story says. Look for the logic behind your child's spellings. The spelling "kn" for "can" makes sense—it's how the word sounds—and actually shows great phonemic understanding. Rest assured that as your child gains experience in both reading and writing words, she will come closer to standard spelling. In the meantime, check the activities in the Reading Exercises of this book to reinforce her ability to hear—and therefore write—letter sounds (see page 83) and remember sight words (see page 98).

Most second graders are in the transitional spelling stage. In this stage, children write words with both vowels and consonants, though the exact vowels they use sometimes seem to have been chosen at random. Spellings during this stage can vary greatly. Some children rely heavily on practice spelling (also called invented spelling, temporary spelling, or transitional spelling). Many still spell most words exactly as they sound. Other children seem rule-bound and are quick to generalize anything they learn about spelling. If this week's spelling list contains words with two vowels together, then suddenly every word these children write has to have two vowels.

Gradually, if they have enough practice writing, children in the transitional spelling stage include greater numbers of standard spellings and sight words in their writing. The pieces they write are longer (five or more sentences) and flow more easily than they did in the previous stage. Writers in this stage begin to use—in fact, many adore—punctuation at the end of their sentences. Stories pop up in which every sentence ends with an exclamation point or a question mark. Capitalization of the first word in a sentence, the pronoun *I*, and proper names becomes more consistent.

Writing in the Classroom

Does writing improve by magic? No, it improves with practice. In a good second grade classroom, children write all the time and for different reasons. They write about science experiments they have performed, field trips they have taken, books they have read, what they plan to do each day, and how everything turned out at the end of the day. They write stories, poems, plays, and cartoon captions. They also study *how* to write. Blocks of time are set aside so that children can generate ideas and choose a topic, plan what they want to say, and write it all out so that people can read it. The mechanics of writing—penmanship, spelling, punctuation—are taught in small groups or during individual conferences as the need arises. Students share drafts with classmates and the teacher, revise their work according to others' suggestions and eventually publish their work in school-made books or on the bulletin board for others to read.

If your child's writing program is like the one described above, do not assume that every piece your child writes will be perfected, or even revised.

What comes home in your child's backpack may be a page of random ideas about penguins, a first draft of a story with the sentences numbered to show a logical sequence, or a finished poem that your child has decorated with illustrations. Naturally you will be impressed by the perfect final piece, but don't overlook the hard work and good thinking that went into the rough drafts and revisions. Learning to write well is a long process. Your child needs to know that you are behind her every step of the way.

Writing at Home

In first grade your child's major writing task was just getting the words onto paper. In second grade she is expected to write longer, more detailed pieces, aiming for complete sentences, standard spelling, and more uniform handwriting. You can help her in three general ways.
1. By giving her lots of informal, real-world opportunities to write.
2. By supporting her classroom spelling program.
3. By watching out for stumbling blocks.
With your help, your second grader can become a confident writer, *but do not push too hard.* Your goal is to keep your child writing for pleasure and with enthusiasm. If sometime next summer your child suddenly says, "Let's make a book about that!" or "We can make a list," then you will know that you have done a magnificent job.

Providing Opportunities to Write

Keep in mind that your child will learn to write only by writing. Your job at home is to do what you always have done: keep him writing. More than anything, your child needs to know that writing is useful; it can even be fun. He needs to know that what he has to say is important—especially that it is important to you. (For additional ideas, see page 84.)

HAVE FIVE MINUTES?

➤ Provide a place for your child to write. Most second graders love to create special places. Offer to help your child arrange an office where he can draw, write, and do his homework and other business. Set up a desk or table in his room or a quiet corner of the house. Your child will be more than happy to make a sign—Private! Keep Out!—to establish his territorial rights.

➤ Second graders also love *stuff.* At this age children have fun collecting school supplies and stocking their home office. You'll find many supplies—pencils, markers, and paper and stationery—already lying around your home. Others you can buy inexpensively at discount department or office supply stores.

➤ Keep reading aloud. Jane Yolen, a well-known children's author, once said, "I have two pieces of advice for young people interested in writing: read and write. Read and read and read." The more children read and are read to, the more familiar they will become with a huge variety of writing forms, the music of language, and a sense of story. Reading good writing can also be inspirational. A second grader who has just read *Nate the Great* by Marjorie Weinman Sharmat (Coward) may be inspired to write his own detective story featuring, of course, himself. A child who has had *Anastasia Krupnik* by Lois Lowry (Houghton Mifflin) read to him recently may decide to keep his own lists of Things I Love and Things I Hate. As for *Alexander and the Terrible, Horrible, No Good, Very Bad Day* (Judith Viorst, Atheneum), what could be more inspiring than a terrible, horrible day?

➤ Second graders love their privacy, and many will relish the thought of keeping a diary or journal. A diary with a lock and key makes a great gift, but a small spiral notebook works just as well. Though few second graders have the stamina or discipline for daily writing, most like the idea of having one place where they can write their innermost feelings and secrets. Be sure to let your child know that he can write or draw *anything* in his journal and that *you will not peek.* (That's the hard part!)

➤ Write lists, lists, and more lists. Your child probably sees you making lists all the time: shopping lists, to-do lists, lists of business accounts, packing lists. Perhaps that's why children of this age are such great list-makers. Encourage your child to make lists of all kinds, from the practical (Things I Need for School), to the personal (Things My Brother Does to Bug Me), to the political (Rules for Using My Tape Recorder), to the fanciful (Ten Ways to Comb Your Hair When You Don't Have a Comb).

List making can be a parent's best friend during this age of complaints and fears. Your teacher isn't fair? Make a list of the things he does wrong. You suddenly hate your best friend? List the reasons why. Overburdened with household duties? Write down a list of your chores and we'll talk about it.

➤ Set up mailboxes for each family member near the front door or in some other convenient place. Lesson or practice reminders, "Hurray for you!" notes, permission slips, and even actual mail can all go into the individual mailboxes for each person to collect.

➤ Your second grader knows that it's not polite to interrupt. So why does he keep interrupting? There's a good chance that he's not trying to be rude; he simply distrusts his ability to remember what he wants to say. If you expect an interruption to be long—if the phone rings or the baby starts to scream—have your second grader write a note to himself about what he wants to say. It may save a great deal of sulking later on!

HAVE MORE TIME?

➤ Publish or perish. The wider the audience your child has for his writing, the more aware he will be of the need for standard writing conventions. Second graders are very practical. Your child knows that although *you* might think his letter about saving the sea otters is brilliant, the editors of your local paper's kids' page won't publish it if they can't read it.

Unfortunately, the streak of perfectionism in many seven- to eight-year-olds sometimes gets in the way. It's nearly impossible for a second grader to think about spelling, handwriting, *and* what he wants to say at the same time. One mistake on a thank-you note can lead to frustration, tears, and pages of crumpled-up stationery. One way to avoid this problem is to get your child in the habit of writing a quick first draft of anything that will go to the outside world, even a postcard. You and he can go over the draft for mistakes before he copies the message onto the postcard or into the pages of a handmade book.

Every time your child writes for a public audience, he is publishing. The list of "publishing" opportunities is endless:
- postcards to friends (even in-town friends will love getting mail)
- thank-you notes, holiday greetings, get-well cards
- letters to relatives, authors, toy companies, or even to the president
- gift books—a gardening journal for Grandpa, an ABC book for the baby, a joke book or comic book for a friend in the hospital, books of baseball statistics or jump-rope rhymes for cousins
- E-mail
- instructions for a homemade board game
- map or directions to an important place
- instructions for the baby-sitter
- notes to the teacher (make sure you sign it)
- posters, buttons, and bumper stickers

➤ There is no better way to honor your child's writing than to shape it into a handmade book. By this time, your child probably knows how to make simple books by stapling pages together with a construction-paper cover. Is it a book about soccer? Make it in the shape of a soccer ball. Or, for a special treat, take your child's masterpiece to a copy shop and have it spiral- or comb-bound.

➤Keep a poetry notebook. Read your second grader a poem from Shel Silverstein's *Where the Sidewalk Ends* (HarperCollins) or Jack Prelutsky's *A Pizza the Size of the Sun* (Greenwillow), and he will collapse into fits of giggles. If you mention the poem a few days later, however, he may not be able to find it. From a second grader's point of view individual poems are pretty small, but collections of poetry are very big. Suggest that your child choose some poems he particularly likes and copy them into a loose-leaf binder. If he balks at copying them out, it will take only minutes for you to write or type them for him. As he adds to his collection, he may be inspired to write down playground rhymes and poems of his own to keep with the others. The following books contains old favorites and new gems to enjoy:
  • *An Arkful of Animals,* selected by William Cole (Houghton Mifflin)
  • *A Book of Pigericks* and other books by Arnold Lobel (Harper & Row)
  • *Every Time I Climb a Tree* and other books, by David McCord (Little, Brown)
  • *Hailstones and Halibut Bones* by Mary O'Neill (Doubleday)
  • *I Saw You in the Bathtub and Other Folk Rhymes,* by Alvin Schwartz (HarperTrophy)
  • *A Light in the Attic* and other books, by Shel Silverstein (Harper & Row)
  • *Honey, I Love,* by Eloise Greenfield (Harperfestival)
  • *The Random House Book of Poetry for Children,* selected by Jack Prelutsky (Random House)
  • *Something Big Has Been Here* and other books, by Jack Prelutsky (Greenwillow)
  • *Yours Till Banana Splits: 201 Autograph Rhymes,* by Joanna Cole and Stephanie Calmenson (Beech Tree)

➤Few second graders can resist a treasure hunt. Have your child set one up for a friend, a sibling, or you.

➤Explore a passion while it lasts. Your second grader may stun you with his in-depth knowledge of California condors, record-breaking football players, or dread diseases. Before he moves on to another interest, help him make a fact book about his current love.

Supporting Your Child's Spelling Program

Second grade spelling programs differ from state to state, school to school, and even classroom to classroom. In some second grades, spelling continues to be taught within the context of the reading and writing program. In most, however, some sort of formal spelling program is initiated. Some teachers make up individualized spelling lists from their students' writing journal. Others create lists based on words the children are learning in reading, science or social studies. Other classrooms use spelling workbooks with weekly lists that must be memorized. Check with your child's teacher. The more you know about your child's spelling program, the more you will be able to help her.

It is worth noting that word attack skills and spelling skills are two sides of the same coin. See the activities beginning on page 83 for additional ways to reinforce your child's spelling skills.

HAVE FIVE MINUTES?

➤ Make a personal dictionary, file, or poster of words that your child often misspells. It is far easier for your child to look up at a poster to find the spelling of "friend" than to look the word up in a dictionary.

➤ Teach your child how to study a spelling list. Your child's teacher may already have taught your child a method for studying spelling words. If so, try that method first. If not, here is one standard approach:
  1. Have your child write each word on an index card.
  2. Let her sort the cards in any way that makes sense to her. Ask her if there are any similarities among the words. Do many of them start with *th,* for example, or contain a silent *e?*
  3. Give your child a pretest. Say each word and have her spell it aloud or write it down. Put any words she knows in a separate pile.
  4. Have your child study the remaining words. Talk about each word. Say, for example, "What do you already know about this word? How many syllables does this word have?" Then let your child say each word aloud and write it on a sheet of paper.
  5. Test her again. Put aside any words she now knows, and repeat step 4 with the others.

➤ Make sure your child has a good picture dictionary. It's possible that she has been reading her picture dictionary for years. Now is the time to reintroduce it to her in a new light. Remind your second grader that she can use her dictionary to check spellings and show her how. You might also want to look in the library or bookstore for dictionaries and word books that are organized in ways other than alphabetical order.

➤ At a restaurant or in the car, use your child's spelling words to play Hangman. In fact, play Hangman anytime with any category of words. It's great spelling practice.

HAVE MORE TIME?

➤ If your child is bringing home spelling lists, and study methods like the one mentioned above aren't working, your child may need to go about this task a different way. Not everybody learns in the same way. Some people need to see something before they can commit it to memory. Others need to hear it. Still others need to *do* it. You may already have a pretty good idea of how your child learns best. If not, help your child to pick and choose from the following list of activities until she finds one that works for her.

VISUAL STRATEGIES
- Write the word in one color. Then close your eyes and visualize the word in that color.
- Write the word in large letters on an index card. Cut around the word so that you can see the shape of the word.

- Find the word in magazines, newspapers, or junk mail. Circle it or cut it out.

KINESTHETIC OR TACTILE STRATEGIES
- Write the word in shaving cream, in salt on a cookie sheet, or in the sand or mud in your yard.
- Write the word in huge letters in the air.
- Use magnetic letters or letter cards to spell the word.
- Use a flashlight to spell the word on a darkened wall.
- Have someone trace the letters of a word on your back. Guess what the word is. Then switch roles.
- Draw the word in giant chalked letters on the pavement, or use masking tape on the floor. Walk, skip, or hop along the letters.

AUDITORY STRATEGIES
- Say the word slowly, emphasizing the hard letter sounds. If a word has silent letters, you might want to sound them out (*k-nife*) so that you will remember them.

- As you write the word, say each letter aloud.
- Sing the word to a familiar tune:
  S-h-a-p-e, s-h-a-p-e,
  Heigh-ho the derry-o, s-h-a-p-e.
- Play word games, like Scrabble, Boggle, and Spill & Spell, with your child to strengthen her awareness of words and spelling skills.
- Use your child's spelling words to make simple crossword or word-find puzzles. Then challenge her to make one for you!

Watching Out for Stumbling Blocks

Sadly, no matter how enthusiastic you are and no matter how many writing opportunities you provide, you can't guarantee that your second grader will become a confident writer. Some children seem to hate writing from the very start. They are impatient with the task of forming letters, or they just can't come up with anything to say. What's the problem?

First of all, look at your child's individual progress in language skills. Is she trying out new vocabulary in her speech? Is she reading more fluently, or finding new ways to figure out words she doesn't know? If your child's reading or language skills as a whole seem to be at a standstill or lagging behind those of her classmates, ask her teacher to refer you to the appropriate support services. In nearly all school districts, testing and support services are available *whether your child is enrolled in public school or not.*

On the other hand, if your child seems to be progressing well in her language skills but balks at writing, perhaps she has hit a stumbling block. The two stumbling blocks that commonly plague second graders are

1. Concern that their work isn't good enough
2. Difficulty with handwriting

E. B. White, the author of *Charlotte's Web,* once said, "I admire anybody who has the guts to write at all." Putting words on paper takes courage and stamina. (Think about the last time you had to write an important business proposal or letter.) For the careworn second grader who can't seem to make the transition from brilliant thoughts to well-constructed paragraphs or whose fine motor skills still need strengthening, writing can seem a fearful and wearisome task. Fortunately, there are many ways you can help make this task seem less risky and tiresome.

HAVE FIVE MINUTES?

➤ One of the scary things about writing is that it seems so permanent. At school your child may erase and erase, but she knows that eventually all that erasing is going to wear a hole in her paper. At home you can ease this concern by giving your child a chalkboard, dry marker board, or Magnadoodle to write on. Any of these will allow her to start over and over with a "clean slate." If you have a home computer with a word processing program, show your child how to insert and delete text. She may spend hours just changing and rearranging her story!

➤ Give your second grader a chance to draw. Drawing was one of your child's first attempts at written communication. It is still a great way to spark ideas, organize thoughts, and build small motor strength. Unfortunately, many second grade writing programs leave drawing behind, or they have children draw pictures *after* the stories are written (as illustrations) rather than before (as inspiration). Talk about the pictures your child draws and encourage her to build stories around them. Then, when she is stuck for a writing idea, suggest that she use one of her "drawing stories."

➤ If your child has difficulty coming up with ideas of her own, encourage her to retell a story from a book she knows well. From this point of safety, she may decide that she can elaborate a bit on the story by changing the ending or adding a character. Eventually, she may come up with a completely new episode of her own.

➤ Suggest that your child follow patterns from predictable books or familiar rhymes. This is a technique that even professional writers have been known to use. Think of Laura Joffe Numeroff's *If You Give a Mouse a Cookie* and *If You Give a Moose a Muffin* or Lewis Carroll's "Twinkle twinkle little bat, How I wonder where you're at." Check the list of predictable books on page 73, or make up patterns of your own.

➤ Give your child alternative writing tools. Many second graders tend to grip their pencils tightly and form tiny letters. Fat primary pencils may feel awkward and uncomfortable now, and trying to fill the guidelines on primary paper may seem more like drawing than writing. If your child's grip seems particularly awkward, you might want to have her try a pencil grip or a three-sided pencil.

HAVE MORE TIME?

➤ Record your child's story. Many second graders (and adults) have a hard time thinking and writing at the same time. Your child might prefer to tape-record his story before writing it. He can then stop, rewind, and play the story as many times as he needs to as he transfers the words to paper.

➤ Writing takes imagination. Remember and reinforce the power of the imagination. Give your child ample time, space, and materials for free play. Provide dress-up clothes, large boxes, wood and carpentry tools, and water, sand, and snow to encourage those creative juices to flow.

➤ Do projects that develop small motor skills. Sewing, carpentry, and arts and crafts projects all strengthen muscles that your child needs for writing. Libraries and bookstores have shelves full of craft books for children, but do understand the joy of free play and experimentation as well.

➤ Play with poetry forms. A definite structure can be a comfort to children who have difficulty writing. You might even want to try some of these simple formats yourself!

- *Name poems.* Use the letters in a name to begin each line of poetry:
  Great cook.
  Reads all the time.
  Always smiles.
  Never yells.
- *Pattern poems:*

sand	(subject)
hot, gritty	(2 words that describe it)
blows, shifts, sinks	(3 words that tell what it does)
gets stuck between your toes	(a thought about the subject)
sand	(same word or synonym)

- *Shape poems.* Write words in different shapes:

➤ Use the tactile strategies listed on page 113 to give your child practice in forming letter shapes.

Reading and Writing Enrichment

If you peek into a second grade classroom during independent reading time, you will probably see a wide range of reading materials. Some children will be mouthing the memorized words of *I Know an Old Lady Who Swallowed a Fly* or sounding out the phonic patterns in *Sam and the Firefly*. Others will be poring over beginning chapter books like *Fox and His Friends*. Still others will be deeply absorbed in *James and the Giant Peach* or *Charlotte's Web*. Students' stories on the wall also show a wide range of writing skills. Some are little more than a few loosely connected sentences. Others are full-blown stories with lively characterization and plot. Most probably fall somewhere in between.

You may find that your child's abilities fall into her class's upper range in reading or writing, or both. If so, you may feel relieved—"Well, at least we don't have to worry about that!" Before you decide that you don't need to be concerned about reading and writing, however, think about the skills your child is still building:

- reading and writing fluency
- an imaginative approach to print
- vocabulary growth
- higher-level comprehension and thinking skills
- an appreciation of the sounds, rhythms, textures, and uses of words
- an increasing desire to read a variety of print

To continue to grow as a reader and writer, your child will need your support both in school and out. Even the best teachers can find their time and energy taken up helping children at the lower end of the skill spectrum. Your child deserves to be supported and challenged with materials that suit her abilities. Find out as much as you can about how and what your child is reading and writing in school by asking questions.

Does my child have access to books that interest and challenge her?

If your child's school or classroom is lacking in resources, offer to send books in with your child. Some libraries have special programs for long-term lending to classrooms. Work with your child's teacher, school administration, or parent-teacher organization to find sources of free and inexpensive reading materials.

Can my child approach this assignment another way?

Perhaps your child would like to start writing a chapter book during her independent writing time, or maybe she would like to read David Macaulay's *The Way Things Work* in addition to the science book chapter on simple machines. Most second graders assume that rules are unbendable: "We have to write about our pets," or "I'm supposed to read this chapter." Your child may need your help in learning how to approach her teacher with alternative ideas.

Are there times when my child can get together with other children who have similar abilities and interests?

Reading *The Black Stallion* can be a lonely experience if everybody else in the classroom is reading *Danny and the Dinosaur*. See if your child can be paired with a reading buddy on the same reading level. Ask if children from different classrooms can get together to share ideas about reading and writing. Suggest starting a school-sponsored book club or writers' group.

What other resources are available for my child?

Support services, gifted and talented programs, and extracurricular activities may be available that will greatly enrich your child's reading and writing experiences. Check with your child's teacher, the school administration, or the district office to find out what they are.

Above all, keep in mind that your child is learning a lot more than academic subjects in her second grade classroom. She is learning self-control and organizational skills. She is learning how to get along in a group and how to negotiate a wide variety of relationships with other children and with adults. These skills, as well as skill in reading and writing, are vital to your child's success in school—and in life. Even if your child is reading *The Secret Garden* on her own, she still needs time to giggle over the antics of George and Martha with her friends. Activities like the ones below will help your child stay interested and challenged in reading and writing. But don't forget to give her time to play freely as well. Remember, as sophisticated as she tries to be, she's still a little kid.

HAVE FIVE MINUTES?

➤ Keep reading aloud to your child. Even the most proficient second grade reader still spends a lot of time figuring out the words. Reading aloud gives you a chance to stir your child's imagination and help her develop a sense of language and story. It also gives you an opportunity to help her increase her vocabulary and comprehension skills, and it allows you to demonstrate correct pronunciation and expressive oral reading.

➤ Be playful with words. Always be on the lookout for a good pun: "Boy, that old kennel is really going to the dogs. Get it?" Even if your child doesn't get it right away, she will come to understand that it's fun to play with words. There are a number of delightfully wacky books for children about the vagaries of the English language. Use them to inspire your own wordplay.
  • *A Cache of Jewels, and Other Collective Nouns,* by Ruth Heller (Grosset and Dunlap)
  • *cdb!,* by William Steig (Simon & Schuster)
  • *Easy as Pie: A Guessing Game of Sayings,* by Marcia Folsom and Michael Folsom (Clarion)
  • *Eight Ate: A Feast of Homonym Riddles,* by Marvin Terban (Clarion)
  • *Mad as a Wet Hen! And Other Funny Idioms,* by Marvin Terban (Clarion)
  • *What's a Frank Frank? Tasty Homograph Riddles,* by Giuilo Maestro (Clarion)
  • *What's in a Word? A Dictionary of Daffy Definitions,* by Rosalie Moscovitch (Houghton Mifflin)

➤ Pass time in the car by building sentences. Write down a two-word sentence (subject and verb). Then take turns adding one word to the sentence without changing the order of the words. The last person to add a word is the winner. Here's an example:
School starts.
School starts early.
School starts early tomorrow.

Our school starts early tomorrow.
Luckily, our school starts early tomorrow.
Luckily, our school starts early tomorrow afternoon.

➤ Make a fact file. Keep a recipe box or shoe box full of index cards in the kitchen or in some other common area. Each time you or your child runs across an interesting fact, write it on a card and keep it in the file. Facts can come from anywhere—books, newspapers, radio, television, school, office, or the barbershop. Fact cards can serve as story starters, report topics, conversation peppers, or boredom busters: "Hey, did you know that you have fewer bones when you're an adult than you did when you were born? Why do you suppose that happens? How can we find out?"

➤ Read *Nothing Ever Happens on 90th Street* by Roni Schotter (Orchard). Then send your child out to sit on your front stoop and record what happens.

➤ Reread a familiar story and talk about how the characters solved the conflict in the tale. Then ask your child to come up with an alternative solution to the conflict: "How else could the three pigs have gotten rid of the wolf?" or "What if the woodsman hadn't been nearby? Then what would Red Riding Hood have done?" Have her write, perform, or create a comic strip showing the alternate solution.

➤ Speak in abbreviations. You might ask, for example, "What kind of cookies do you want to make tomorrow? CCC's?" It may take your second grader a moment, but she'll be very pleased with herself when she figures out that "CCC" means "chocolate chip cookies."

HAVE MORE TIME?

➤ Make your child the editor of the family newspaper. Look through the local paper to figure out what kinds of writing should be included: feature articles, letters to the editor, classified ads, sports scores, advice columns, comics, and so on. Have your editor make writing assignments (be sure she takes one or two on herself) and set deadlines. When the time comes, help her lay out the paper on sheets of butcher paper or type the articles into a newsletter format on your home computer.

➤ Put on a family play or talent show. Put your second grader in charge of writing the script, designing programs, or making cue cards. Videotape the show if possible. Assign your child the role of critic and have her write up a review of opening night.

➤ Encourage your child to enter a contest. Check local newspapers, children's magazines, toy stores, and bookstores for contests suitable for seven- to eight-year-olds. *The Ultimate Guide to Student Contests, Grades K–6* by Scott Pendleton (Walker) lists contests like the Jabberwocky Poetry Contest for young children.

➤ Nurture an inventor. Challenge your child to come up with something new and exciting. How about a brand-new sport or a machine that will make your bed for you? Have her make a plan for a new invention with an explanation of how it words. If the plan looks good, try to build it!

➤ Ask your child to help you make up a family code. Then use it to write secret messages for lunch boxes, briefcases, and other surprising places. Your library should have plenty of books about codes to help you get started.

➤ Hook your child up with a pen pal. Ask people you know if they have friends or relatives with children who live in another part of the country or the world. Call your church or local service organizations. Check your library for lists of professional organizations that match pen pals by age and language. If you have a home computer, perhaps your child can become the key pal of a classmate or friend.

➤ Suggest that your child use graph paper or construction toys to design a city. Have her write a constitution for the city. Who are the city's officials? What are the city's laws? What happens when someone breaks a law? You may gain great insight into your second grader's sense of law and order!

➤ Encourage your child to submit work for publication. Many children's magazines publish artwork, writing, and photography by children.

For publishers of children's writing, look in your library for *Market Guide for Young Writers* by Kathy Henderson (Writer's Digest).

➤ If your second grader reads well enough to move on to children's novels, you will find plenty of choices available. At any library or large bookstore you will finds shelves and shelves of paperbacks labeled "Middle Grade Fiction." Do be somewhat selective, however, as you help your second grader choose books to read. Your child may read at the fifth grade level, but that doesn't mean she has the emotional maturity of a fifth grader. Try to steer clear of books that deal with the trials and tribulations of an older child's life. Instead, look for books, like the ones listed below, to enrich the life of your second grader right now. (See also the list of books on page 68.)

- *Abel's Island,* by William Steig (Farrar, Straus, & Giroux)
- *Amber Brown Is Not a Crayon* and other books by Paula Danziger (Scholastic)
- The Bunnicula series, by Deborah and James Howe (Atheneum)
- *Catwings,* by Ursula K. Le Guin (Orchard)
- *Cricket in Times Square,* by George Sheldon (Farrar, Straus & Giroux)
- The Encyclopedia Brown series, by Donald J. Sobol (Nelson)
- *Freckle Juice,* by Judy Blume (Four Winds)
- *How to Eat Fried Worms,* by Thomas Rockwell (Franklin Watts)
- The Littles series, by John Peterson (Scholastic)
- *Mr. Popper's Penguins,* by Richard and Florence Atwater (Little, Brown)
- *Pippi Longstocking,* by Astrid Lingren (Viking)
- *The Shrinking of Treeborn,* by Florence Parry Heide (Holiday)
- *Wolf Story,* by William McCleery (Shoestring Press)

Math Exercises

Number Sense

The ability to understand number is measured by questions 1 and 2 on the Math Assessment.

"Math." The very word conjures up visions of heads bent over ditto sheets, pencils with chewed erasers gripped in sweaty hands. No wonder the word has the power to strike terror in a parent's heart, even the parent of a second grader. You might wonder how on earth you're going to get your child through subtraction with borrowing, let alone through the long division, fractions, and decimals that are yet to come. Try to relax. You have more going for you than you might realize. Your child started school with a wealth of mathematical knowledge gained from years of playing with objects and observing the world around her. And every time she pours a glass of milk, plays a game of checkers, or shares a package of M&M's with a friend, she is continuing to build that knowledge.

The knowledge that your child already has, and that she continues to build upon, is known as number sense. This number sense—an understanding of quantity and the way numbers work—is at the very heart of the computation and estimation skills your child will be learning this year. The more experience she has working with concrete numbers, the more mathematical understanding she will have, and the easier computation, measurement, and other math skills will be for her.

Your child will most likely be doing more work this year with mathematical symbols such as the plus, minus, and multiplication signs. This does not mean that she no longer needs hands-on experience. On the contrary, she needs it now more than ever. If your child's experience with math is limited to paper and pencil, she will learn math as a series of tricks or procedures and will have no real understanding to build upon in the future. She may get through simple addition and subtraction, but she will not have the mental strength to tackle concepts like multiplication or division. To build a strong foundation of understanding, she needs to have concrete mathematical experiences now, and lots of them. This is where you come in. For more activities that will reinforce your child's number sense, see page 130.

HAVE FIVE MINUTES?

➤ Continue to count objects and actions: How many times can you jump rope? How many people are in the line for ice cream? How many dirty socks can you find under your bed? How many white cars are in this parking lot? How many blue cars? How many purple-striped cars? (Don't forget zero.)

➤ Make counting a game by estimating first. Then ask your child to count to see whose estimate is closest.

➤ Ask number riddles, such as these:
  • What number comes after 1000?
  • What numbers are greater than 14 but less than 20?
  • What's the largest number you can make with the digits 2, 4, and 6?

➤ Show your own interest in numbers by pointing out interesting numbers and their uses in your daily life. Talk about how *you* use numbers. When you are keeping track of prices at the grocery store, do you estimate or do you calculate? How about when you're keeping track of a basketball score? When you read that the University of Michigan stadium holds 105,000 people, what does that mean to you? Instead of saying "I'm not good at estimating the size of a crowd," ask your child's help in figuring out strategies that will help you.

➤ Count backwards. You may be surprised at how challenging this can be. (Quick, count back from 500 million!) Counting backwards is more than a trick. Among other things, it is the basis for subtraction. Here are some ways to fit this activity into your day:

- Will the school bus come before your second grader can count back from 100?
- If you can stand it (and you probably can't), let your child sing "99 Bottles of Beer on the Wall," starting with 999.

➤ Draw a dot-to-dot pattern on the back of your place mat at a restaurant. Number the dots with a series of numbers that will challenge your child: 20 to 50 or 375 to 400 or 1,000 to 1,040, for example. Have your child complete the picture. Then challenge her to create a similar dot-to-dot puzzle for you.

➤ Pick a number between 0 and 10. Invite your child to guess the number. With each guess, tell her whether your number is less than or greater than her guess. For example, if your number is 7 and she guesses 3, you say, "No, it is greater than 3." Keep track of the number of guesses your child takes and challenge her to beat her record in the next round. You can play this game using any set of numbers, as long as your child is comfortable with the counting range.

➤ "Get in that bathtub before I count to ten!" Sound familiar? Any time you find yourself counting to get something done—bedtime, chore time, putting-shoes-on time—skip-count instead. Each time your child hears you count by threes, fives, twenties, or hundreds, he is learning about number patterns.

➤ Use ordinal numbers. Hang a calendar in your child's room, and talk about the days: "Today is June sixth" or "Sam's party is on April fourteenth." Be aware of using ordinal numbers in daily conversation: "Who is third in your team's lineup?" and "Which errand do you want to do first? What do you want to do second?" Ask questions involving ordinal numbers: "What is the tenth letter of the alphabet?"

➤ Whenever you are counting change, demonstrate skip-counting. Encourage your child to count pennies by twos, nickels by fives, and dimes by tens.

HAVE MORE TIME?

➤ Talk about the words "even" and "odd." Ask if numbers you run into are even or odd. If necessary, give your second grader this tip: "If the number ends in 0, 2, 4, 6, or 8, it is even. If it ends in 1, 3, 5, 7, or 9, it is odd."

If your child has a hard time remembering the numbers 0, 2, 4, 6, and 8, you might show him this trick: "Take the number 6. Try to use your fingers to make 6 so that you show the same number of fingers on each hand. If you can, the number is even."

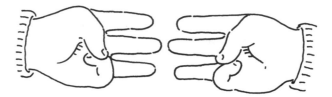

➤ Play board games. This is a second grader's version of a preschooler's "read to me!" They guarantee involvement with Mom or Dad. Any board game in which the players move ahead by tossing a die or turning a spinner gives practice in counting forward, a precursor to the addition strategy of "adding on." Some commercial games are particularly well suited to reinforcing number sense. Here are just a few:

Battleship
Card games of any sort
Checkers
Chess
Chinese checkers
Mancala
Parcheesi
Tangrams
Uno
Yahtzee

➤ Waiting for your food at a restaurant? Play Count Up, using twenty sugar packets or toothpicks. Tell your child that you will take turns placing one or two sugar packets on the table. The person who places the last sugar packet is the winner.

As your child becomes more comfortable with this game, you can try it without sugar packets (an easier version for the car). Count from 1 to 20, taking turns counting one or two numbers. For example, your child may start with 1; you say 2, 3; she says 4, 5; you say 6; and so on. The person who says 20 wins. For this version, you can use any spread of numbers, such as 44 to 64 or 725 to 745.

➤Teach your child to play solitaire. It reinforces sequencing as well as strategy skills.

➤Read aloud books about basic number concepts. New counting books are published each year that reinforce number concepts and counting skills in new ways. Here are some particularly good choices.
  • *Anno's Math Games,* by Anno Mitsumasa (Philomel)
  • *How Many Stars in the Sky?,* by Lenny Hort (Tambourine)
  • *How Much Is a Million?,* by David Schwartz (Scholastic)
  • *A Million Fish . . . More or Less,* by Patricia McKissack (Knopf)
  • *Two Ways to Count to Ten: A Liberian Folktale,* by Ruby Dee (Holt)
  • *When Sheep Cannot Sleep,* by Satoshi Kitamura (Farrar, Straus & Giroux)

➤Play Morra, a game that dates back to the Middle Ages. To play, each player hides one hand. On the signal, "Morra," the players show their hands with a number of fingers outstretched and call out "Even" or "Odd." If the total number of fingers showing is an even number, the player who called "Even" wins. If it is an odd number, the player who called "Odd" wins. Of course, if both players call the same thing, they both either win or lose.

Place Value

The ability to recognize the meaning of hundreds, tens, and ones is measured by questions 6 and 7 in the Math Assessment.

You may suppose that if your child can count to one hundred, she has mastered the concepts behind place value and our base-ten number system. Don't be fooled. To understand place value, your child must know how to make groups of ten objects and then count those groups as if each group were just one. She must understand that a digit can mean something different depending upon where it is placed in a number—for example, the meaning of 8 is very different in the numbers 18, 83, 845, and 8,729. These are sophisticated concepts. In fact, place value may be one of the most difficult subjects your child will have to tackle in elementary school—and she will do most of this work by the end of second grade.

The single best way to reinforce your child's understanding of place value is to give her lots of practice counting and grouping concrete materials. Many children learn to add and subtract two-digit numbers in second grade by "carrying the one" or "borrowing from the eight." Chances are, your child will learn these procedures this year, too. A good strong understanding of place value will give your child a leg up as she tackles not only addition and subtraction but multiplication, division, and decimals as well. To help give her that boost, use concrete activities like the ones below.

Many teachers use manipulatives such as base ten blocks to help their students learn about place value. Base-ten blocks, Cuisenaire rods, and interlocking cubes such as Unifix cubes are available at toy stores and through educational supply catalogs. You can also use the patterns on page 192 to make base-ten blocks from sturdy construction paper. A complete set should contain at least 10 hundreds (flats), 30 tens (rods or longs), and 60 ones (units).

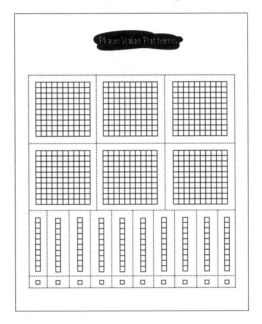

HAVE FIVE MINUTES?

➤ How many smiling faces can you draw in one minute? Time each other and count the results by circling groups of ten faces.

➤ Play Dots. Have your child make lots and lots of dots on a piece of paper. Then take turns circling groups of ten. The last person to circle a group of ten is the winner. After all the groups of ten have been circled, have your child count the groups of ten and the ones left over and tell you the total number of dots. Write the number on the paper so that she can see its written form.

➤ Whenever you are doing chores such as bundling together recyclables or picking up sticks in the yard after a storm, make bundles of ten. Then group those tens into hundreds, if possible.

HAVE MORE TIME?

➤ You and your child can use beans and craft sticks to make inexpensive base-ten manipulatives. Use the beans as ones (also called *units*). Glue ten beans along one craft stick to make a bean stick of ten (also called a *rod* or a *long*). Then glue ten craft sticks together on a piece of cardboard (cereal box cardboard is perfect) to make a bean flat of one hundred (also called a *flat*). Start with nine of each size, though you may find that you need to make more as you go along.

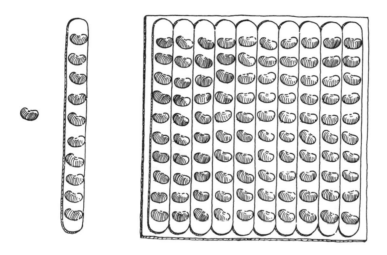

➤ Use the base ten blocks to build numbers for your child to "read." Show her 1 hundred, 3 tens, and 5 ones, and ask her to name the number shown. Write down the number so that you can both see it on paper.

➤ Place play money in piles of hundred-dollar bills, ten-dollar bills, and one-dollar bills. Take turns rolling a die and taking that number of ones from the pile, exchanging ten ones for one ten and ten tens for one hundred whenever possible. The first person to get a one-hundred-dollar bill wins.

➤ Play Make a Number. The object of this game is to make and read the highest number. Each player makes a game board by drawing four lines on a sheet of paper. Roll a die four times. Each time, the players write the number shown on one of their lines. After they have written all four numbers, the players read their numbers aloud. The player with the highest number wins.

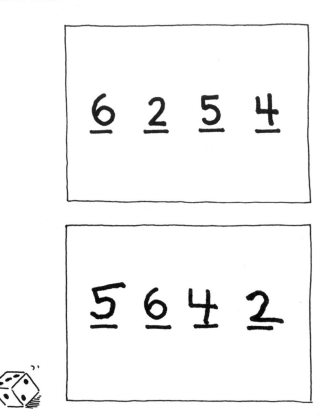

Estimating

The ability to estimate is measured by questions 8 and 9 in the Math Assessment.

Second graders like things to be exact. Most like to list rules and follow rules and come up with the exact right answer. At school, second graders are often expected to come up with the exact right answer as well. Any parent who has watched a second grader erase a hole in his drawing because the cat's mouth wasn't exactly right may understand why estimation or guessing tries the young perfectionist's patience.

Then why encourage a second grader to estimate? Estimation is hard, but it's also very useful. How do you figure out if your car will fit in a parking space or whether you have enough cash to buy the book your child is asking for? Do you get out and measure the parking space or carefully subtract $14.95 from your twenty-dollar bill? Recent research has shown that adults use estimation for as much as half of all their daily arithmetic needs.

For the second grader, estimation has additional importance. A second grader's grasp on number sense is still pretty shaky. (Ask a second grader who doesn't know you how old he thinks you are!) Your child needs repeated experience at guessing and checking numbers to gain a sense of what is reasonable and what is not. If a second grader knows the ages of many of his friends' parents, chances are he will make a pretty good guess at your age. On the other hand, if the only thing he knows is that you have gray hair and so does his granddad, his guess may be quite a bit off the mark.

The ability to figure out if an answer is reasonable or not is a critical computation skill. The child who happily comes up with 410 kids when adding two classes of 25 kids each does not know how to figure out if his answer makes sense. Only experience with estimation will give him the thinking skills he needs to work with numbers sensibly.

Practice estimating with your child whenever you can. Help him understand that not all problems need a correct answer; sometimes a thoughtful guess will do the job just as well. Talk about your reasoning in coming up with your estimations and ask him about his. Every time you do, you will be helping him refine the reasoning skills that are crucial to his success in mathematics.

For additional activities that involve estimation, see Number Sense, page 123; Adding and Subtracting Larger Numbers, page 143; and Measurement, page 154.

HAVE FIVE MINUTES?

➤ No matter where you are, there is probably something handy that you can estimate. How many chairs are in the dentist's waiting room? How many pennies in the family penny jar? How many times a day is the bathroom light left on? How many red lights between here and home?

➤ Do you have a restless second grader hanging about the kitchen while you're trying to prepare dinner? Send him on an estimation hunt. Say, "Hmmm. I wonder how many closets there are in this house." Write down both of your estimates and then send him off to count. Vary your suggestions according to how much time you need. Having a dinner party? Try estimating the number of lightbulbs or furniture legs!

➤ Nothing delights a child more than catching his parent in a mistake. Have your child give you simple story problems that you can solve with a calculator. After every answer, ask, "Does this make sense?" Every now and then hit a button that will throw your calculation way off, so that you come up with 6,666 puppies instead of 6.

➤ Whenever you and your child are waiting for something, estimate how long you will have to wait. Then have your child count (quietly!) to sixty to measure off a minute. Use tally marks or fingers to keep track of the minutes, and see how many minutes he counts off before your wait is over.

➤ Whenever possible, let your child choose plastic containers to store leftovers. Ask, "Do you think all of these noodles will fit in this container?" Even if you are sure they won't fit, let him try it. Your child's mathematical thinking is worth an extra dirty dish or two!

HAVE MORE TIME?

➤ Encourage your child to help out in the kitchen. Cooking with a second grader may not be the most efficient way to get a meal on the table, but the math skill he gains in the process will be well worth the trouble. From soup to nuts, cooking abounds with estimation opportunities: Is there a cup of milk left in the carton? Will the meat and potatoes be done at the same time? Is there enough ice cream for everyone? Is there room in the dishwasher for three more glasses? Help your second grader plan and execute a simple meal for the entire family. You may be pleasantly surprised by the results!

➤ Most likely, your child will not be taught to round numbers off this year. However, the need to round numbers up or down does come up in daily life, usually when estimating prices, weights, or measures. If your child is curious about rounding, use a number line to show him how it's done. Choose a number such as two and ask, "Is two closer to zero or ten on this number line?" After your child has figured out all numbers except five, ask, "Is five closer to zero or ten?" Discuss the problem, and give your child the rule that five is always considered closer to ten. According to your child's developmental stage and personality, he may accept or reject this arbitrary rule!

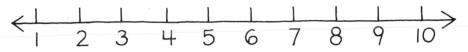

Addition and Subtraction Facts Through 18

The ability to add and subtract numbers through 18 is measured by questions 10 and 11 in the Math Assessment.

It's math time in your child's second grade classroom. At one table some children are building towers with interlocking cubes. On the carpet, some others are playing dominoes. In the reading corner, two children are giggling over a picture book called *Ten in the Bed*. What's going on here?

If your memories of learning math bring visions of flash cards and work sheets, you might look at this scene and wonder, Where is the computation? Where are the math facts? Never fear, the computation is there, even if it is not in a form you immediately recognize.

Basic computation facts are to mathematical reasoning and problem-solving what phonics and sight words are to reading—a useful means to an end. Just as reading is more fluent and enjoyable when one doesn't have to stop to sound out every word, problem-solving is easier and more enjoyable when one doesn't have to stop to figure out each individual fact. Unfortunately, unless your child sees basic computation as a useful skill—like learning to bat a ball so she can play baseball, or how to hammer a nail so she can make a fort—she has a good chance of viewing facts (and math itself) as sheer drudgery.

Most educators agree that children should know their addition and subtraction facts through 18 (that is, $9 + 9 = 18$ and $18 - 9 = 9$) before the end of second grade. With time and plenty of practice, your child will probably be confident of her addition and subtraction facts by the end of the year.

Your second grader will probably spend a fair amount of time at school practicing addition and subtraction facts. If you are lucky, much of this practice will occur in problem-solving situations. You can help your child over the math-facts hump in two ways:

1. *Make addition and subtraction facts a part of your daily life.* Continue to work with concrete materials whenever possible. Learning math facts requires practice, practice, practice. The activities below will help make that practice a little less tiresome.

2. *Teach your child addition and subtraction strategies.* Strategies are not rules. Rules are supposed to be remembered (and are usually easy to forget). A given strategy may or may not help your child get to the answer of a problem. If the strategy helps, great. If not, try another one. You may also find that your child has developed some very interesting strategies of her own. Try not to give the impression that one strategy is

better than another. Any strategy that produces the correct result is a good one.

If your child still uses her fingers to add and subtract basic facts, let her. This simply means that she has not yet committed those facts to memory. Think of fingers as a bridge of comfort. The more comfortable your child is with any given fact, the less often she will need to use her fingers.

Making Addition and Subtraction Facts a Part of Daily Life

HAVE FIVE MINUTES?

➤ Work simple problems into your daily routine. When you are unpacking the groceries, hand the fruit to your child and say, "Here are five apples and six oranges. How many pieces of fruit are going into the refrigerator?" While setting the table, ask, "How many plates are on the table? How many more do we need to make six?"

➤ Make sure your child knows the language of math. A simple statement such as "'Take away' means the same as 'subtract'" may be the "Aha!" that suddenly causes everything to make sense.

➤ Have your child make an addition fact by counting the letters in his name. The name Juan Perez, for example, would become 4 + 5. Try using the names of siblings, friends, and celebrities.

➤ Keep a pair of dice in your purse or in the glove compartment of your car. Whenever you have to wait, take turns tossing the dice and adding the numbers shown. The person with the highest sum—or, if you wish to subtract, the lowest difference—wins the round. If your child is inspired by money, keep the dice in a plastic bag filled with pennies. The winner of each round gets to take a penny from the bag.

Regular dice cover the facts through 12. If you wish to practice higher facts, use masking tape to change the numbers 1, 2, and 3 to 7, 8, and 9. You can also find inexpensive ten-sided dice—bearing the numbers 0 to 9—at toy or hobby shops.

➤ If your child is having difficulty making the transition from working with objects to working with symbols, you might try giving her a handful of counters such as pennies or paper clips. Then write a problem—say,

3 + 2—in vertical form on a sheet of paper. Have your child place the correct number of counters next to each number—that is, three counters next to the 3 and two counters next to the 2. Next, have her collect all the counters and line them up below the answer line. Then ask her to count all the counters and write the result (5) below the line.

$$+\ \frac{3\ 000}{2\ 00}$$

$$+\ \frac{3}{2}$$

$$5\ 000\ 00$$

HAVE MORE TIME?

➤ What is your second grader's current collection passion? Action figures? Stuffed animals? Plastic horses? Rocks? If there's anything your second grader likes right now more than playing with her collection, it's playing with you. Combine the two by taking turns making up addition and subtraction stories about her collection. You might say, "The five crew members are stranded on the dying surface of the planet Zed. What's that, Scottie? The transporter is broken? Oh, no! We can only beam two people back to the starship! How many will be left on Zed?"

➤ Play Hangmath. This game is played just like Hangman, but with numbers instead of letters. Draw a hangman's gallows. Then think of a math fact your child needs to practice—for example, 8 + 9. Draw a playing board showing the placement of the digits in the problem:

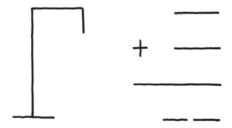

Your child tries to reconstruct the problem by guessing digits. For example, she might guess, "Is there a 9?" If her guess is correct, write the number in the correct position on the playing board. If it is not correct, draw a head on the hanged man. The game ends when your child figures out the problem or when you complete the picture of the hanged man.

➤ Play the game of Sums. You can find commercial versions of this game (Wake Up Giants is one trade name) in toy stores, in catalogs, and often wherever handcrafted wooden toys are sold. Most versions consist of a wooden box with pegs that flip over the numbers and make wonderful gifts. You can also play with dice and pencil and paper. Here's how.

SUMS

1. Write down the numbers 1 to 12 for each player.
2. Players take turns rolling the dice. On each turn, the player may cross out either the sum of the dice or any combination of numbers that equals the sum. For example, a player who rolls a three and a four can cross out 3 and 4, or 7, or 1 and 6, or 2 and 5.
3. Each number may only be crossed out once.
4. When a player cannot play—if, for example, the player has already crossed out 1 through 7—she is out and the sum of the numbers not yet crossed out is her score.
5. When everyone is out, the player with the lowest score wins. For a more difficult variation of the game, you can write down 1 to 18 and use three dice.

➤ Adjust familiar card games to include addition and subtraction. Most second graders adore card games. If the thought of one more game of War or Go Fish makes your eyes cross, try these alternatives. You still might find yourself dozing off, but at least you'll have the comforting knowledge that your child is getting good practice in her math facts:

- Addition or Subtraction War: Remove the face cards from the deck. Deal out all of the remaining cards to the two players. Each player turns over two cards at a time and adds or subtracts their face value (aces count for one). The player with the highest sum or the lowest difference gets all four turned-over cards. When the sums or differences are the same, the players turn over two more cards. The winner gets to take all of the turned-over cards.
- Addition Fish: Remove the face cards and tens from the deck. Play like regular Go Fish, but instead of matching pairs, try to make pairs of numbers that add up to 10.

➤ Play mancala. This African game reinforces all sorts of mathematical thinking, including mental arithmetic. Commercial versions are available, or you can make your own game by using the bottom half of an empty egg carton, two cups or bowls, and 36 beans or stones. Place the egg carton between you and your child. Place an empty cup, or *mancala*, at either end of the carton. The mancala on your right is yours. Here are the rules.

MANCALA

1. Place 3 beans in each egg compartment, leaving the mancalas empty.
2. Players take turns picking up all the beans from an egg compartment on their side and moving them counterclockwise, placing one in each compartment and mancala along their path.
3. If the last bean lands in their own mancala, they take another turn.
4. If the last bean lands in an empty compartment on their side, they put the beans from the opposite compartment into their own mancala.
5. When one player has no more beans left on his side, the game ends. The other player puts all the remaining beans into his mancala. The player with the most beans wins.

Teaching Addition
and Subtraction Strategies

Want to be a hero? To learn the addition facts through 18, your child will have to memorize one hundred facts. Like most children (and adults), your second grader may find the prospect of memorizing one hundred of *anything* mind-boggling. By teaching a few time honored strategies, you can help her gain confidence and speed in learning basic addition and subtraction. They are:

The Fact Family Strategy
$$7 + 8 = 15$$
$$8 + 7 = 15$$
$$15 - 7 = 8$$
$$15 - 8 = 7$$

A child who knows that the numbers 7, 8, and 15 are all related can face a subtraction problem such as 15 − 8 and think, Oh, no! I don't know this one! But wait. I *do* know that 8 + 7 = 15. Does that help? Well, maybe the answer is 7!

The Counting-On and Back Strategy

"Here's one way you can add 6 and 8. Start with the bigger number. Yes, that's 8. Now count on six more numbers: 9, 10, 11, 12, 13, 14. Yes! The answer is fourteen!" Or, "Here's one way you can figure out 17-9. Start with 17. Now count backwards nine numbers: 16, 15, 14, 13, 12, 11, 10, 9, 8. The answer is 8!"

The Doubles, Doubles + 1, and Doubles + 2 Strategies

"7 + 8? That's a tough one. Can you think of a double that's close to 7 + 8?"

"7 + 7 = 14?"

"That's a good one! Now, how much more than 7 is 8?"

"One! Oh, so 7 + 8 is 15!"

The Making-Ten Strategy

"What are you stumped on, 7 + 5? Well, try this: 7 plus 3 equals what?"

"That's easy. 10."

"Okay, so 5 is how many more than 3?"

"That's easy too: 2."

"Okay, so what's 2 more than 10?"

"It's 12! Oh, I get it! 7 plus 5 equals 12!"

HAVE FIVE MINUTES?

➤ Draw or use a domino to demonstrate a fact family. Choose a domino such as the 5/6. Place the domino horizontally in front of your child with the 5 to the left, and say, "Five plus six equals what?" Write down the resulting number sentence. Then cover up the 5 and say, "Eleven minus five equals what?" Again write down the sentence. Then swing the domino around and repeat the process with 6 + 5 and 11 – 6. You can also use playing cards to do this activity.

➤ When you are in the car or waiting in line, give your child three numbers, such as 7, 6, and 13. Have him give you the four related facts that use the numbers given. Then switch roles. When it's your turn to give the facts, try making a mistake now and then, such as 7 – 13 = 6. He'll love it.

➤ To help your child become comfortable with the idea that numbers have different names, challenge your second grader to give you as many different names for a chosen number as he can think of: You might say, for example, "I'm thinking of the number 4. Another name for the number four is 5 – 1. What are some other names?" Allow your child to be as creative as he wants to be. When he is out of suggestions, you may want to add some other possibilities, depending upon his level of understanding:

- the word "four" in another language
- the Roman numeral IV
- four tally marks
- products (2 x 2), quotients (8 ÷ 2), and fractions (**1/2** of 8)

➤At snack time, put a few bite-size snacks in a plastic bag. Give your child a few more and say, "You already have four peanuts in the bag. Here are seven more. How many do you have all together?" Have your child drop the snacks into the bag and count on from the original number to find the total.

➤Look for opportunities for your child to keep a tally in his head: the number of runs in a baseball game, the number of convertibles he sees on a car trip, the number of cans in the grocery basket. Suggest that if he keeps the last number he counted in his head, he can simply count on from it each time a run is scored, a convertible passes, or three more cans are thrown into the grocery basket.

➤Point out doubles that you come across in your daily life. "Does your sister want a snack, too? Okay, double your five Goldfish." Or "How many legs does a spider have? How many are on each side?"

➤In the car, challenge your child to think of all the names for 10 that he can. In a restaurant, write the facts down on the placemat. (There are 9 facts for 10. Can *you* name them all?)

➤Write down one of the columns of addition and subtraction facts related to ten shown below. Ask, "Do you see any patterns?" Talk about how the patterns your child sees could help him remember the facts.

10 + 1 = 11	9 + 1 = 10	18 − 8 = 10
10 + 2 = 12	8 + 2 = 10	17 − 7 = 10
10 + 3 = 13	7 + 3 = 10	16 − 6 = 10
10 + 4 = 14	6 + 4 = 10	15 − 5 = 10
10 + 5 = 15	5 + 5 = 10	14 − 4 = 10
10 + 6 = 16	4 + 6 = 10	13 − 3 = 10
10 + 7 = 17	3 + 7 = 10	12 − 2 = 10
10 + 8 = 18	2 + 8 = 10	11 − 1 = 10
10 + 9 = 19	1 + 9 = 10	

➤Whenever possible, ask questions like this: "You've got six Yankee baseball cards. How many more do you need for ten?" or "Most second graders need ten hours of sleep each night. You slept twelve hours last night. How many more than ten is that?"

➤ Give your child lots of opportunities to use concrete objects to count back. Say to her, for example, "How many potatoes are in the refrigerator? Count back while you hand me four and tell me how many are left."

➤ Encourage your child to use the counting-on strategy to solve everyday problems like these:

- How many jelly beans did I give you? How many did I give your sister? What do I need to do to make things even?
- That game costs about fifteen dollars. How many dollars do you have in your bank? Do you have enough to buy it? How much more do you need?

HAVE MORE TIME?

➤ Most second graders are great record keepers. Send your child off to collect some data about herself or her current passion. Say, for example, "How many of the bugs in your bug collection have wings and how many don't?" or "How many people in our family like Brussels sprouts? How many hate them?" Aske her to make up fact-family stories using the data she has collected.

➤ Use drawing paper and water-based paint to make double-dot pictures. Show your child how to fold the paper in half, then open it up and paint a number of dots (or hearts or butterflies, depending on your child's artistic expertise) on one side. Refold the paper, press the two halves together, and open it again. Notice how the number of dots has doubled. Ask your child to tell you the number sentence that the picture shows—for example, 8 + 8 = 16. For an added challenge, ask your child how he could show 8 + 9 = 17 (by adding one dot to one side of the picture without folding the paper).

➤ Teach your child this variation of the solitaire game called **Pyramid**. With a deck of 52 cards, make a pyramid arrangement beginning with one card and ending with seven. It should look like this:

The object of the game is to remove as many cards from the pyramid arrangement as possible. Here are the rules of the game:

PYRAMID

1. Your goal is to find a pair of numbers that add up to 10 and remove them. You may remove cards only if no other cards overlap them. King, queen, and jack equal ten and may be removed (as can the 10) as soon as they are uncovered.

2. Start by looking in the bottom row for pairs of cards that equal ten. Discard them, and see if any of the remaining uncovered cards make a ten.

3. When you can find no more pairs in the arrangement, go through the remaining deck one card at a time. See if you can use one of the cards in the deck to make a match with an uncovered card in the pyramid. If you can, discard both cards.

4. Count the number of cards left in the pyramid when there are no more matches to make to determine your score. Encourage your child to try to top his previous score each time.

►Play a variation of the card game Concentration. Remove the face cards and tens from a deck of cards. Play a game of Concentration with the remaining cards, but instead of trying to find pairs that match, try to find pairs that add up to ten (aces count as one).

►Play Nim, an ancient Chinese game of strategy. To play this version, start with the number 20. Players take turns subtracting 1, 2, 3, or 4. The player who ends on 0 wins.

►Have your child place a certain number of counters or small toys in a paper bag. Then have her shake the bag, reach in, and pull out a handful of toys. Before counting, have her estimate how many toys might be left in the bag. To confirm her estimate, have her count the toys that she removed and then count on to figure out how many remain in the bag.

Addition and Subtraction with Larger Numbers

The ability to add and subtract larger numbers is measured by questions 12 and 13 in the Math Assessment.

Second grade should come with its own warning: Caution: Borrowing and Carrying Ahead!

Ask any teacher or parent of a former second grader what kids learn in second grade math, and chances are the answer will be "How to carry and borrow." The language might change (current math programs usually talk about "regrouping," "trading," or "exchanging"), but the reality of second grade remains the same. Sometime this year, your child will begin to tackle problems like these:

$$\begin{array}{r} 87 \\ + 69 \\ \hline \end{array} \qquad \begin{array}{r} 346 \\ - 187 \\ \hline \end{array}$$

Few parents have fond memories of learning to add and subtract large numbers. Most of us were taught that there was one right way to add or subtract large numbers—from right to left, borrowing or carrying numbers from one column to another as needed. Most of us eventually figured out what the teacher wanted us to do, but with mixed results in later life. Some of us learned our lessons well—so well, in fact, that when we see the problem $500 - 1 = $ ——, we automatically start crossing out zeros and writing down 9's without thinking that, *of course*, 499 is one less than 500. The rest of us reach for our calculators as soon as we see that a problem has more than three digits.

Math instruction, like reading instruction, is subject to the ebb and flow of educational trends. Many schools are changing the way they introduce children to addition and subtraction. Backed by extensive research, these schools are concluding that the calculation methods most of us learned may fail large numbers of children.

One reason for this failure is that the information explosion and technological advances have changed the type of mathematical work your child will need to do in her life. The mathematical skills your child will most often need are

- the ability to approach a problem and figure out what needs to be done
- the ability to decide what information is needed to solve the problem and figure out how to get any information that's missing
- the ability to look at an answer and decide if it's reasonable

These skills are best gained by approaching messy, everyday, real-life problems over and over again. Work sheets covered with tedious computation problems will not do the trick.

Though computation is still a part of everyday life, your child will probably rely on paper-and-pencil calculations even less than you do today. In addition, those old computation methods we so painstakingly learned can actually cause more harm than good. Most of the mistakes children make in carrying and borrowing are not due to laziness or sloppiness or even a shaky knowledge of math facts. Teachers find that the errors kids make in adding and subtracting large numbers are amazingly consistent. More often than not, these little mathematicians are working just as hard as they can—doggedly applying the right rule in the wrong way. Here are some examples:

$$\begin{array}{r} 16 \\ + 24 \\ \hline 310 \end{array}$$

The child thinks, "Okay, you start on the right, add the numbers in each column, and write the answer below the line."

$$\begin{array}{r} 71 \\ - 25 \\ \hline 54 \end{array}$$

The child thinks, "Subtraction means taking the little number away from the big number."

$$\begin{array}{r} \overset{9\ 9}{5\cancel{0}\cancel{0}} \\ - 174 \\ \hline 425 \end{array}$$

The child thinks, "You can't subtract 4 from 0, so you cross out the zero and make it a nine."

The fact is that there is no one true way of adding and subtracting. Children outside the United States are taught a whole range of different methods, all of which work just as well as methods we were taught as children. You may find that your own child has already come up with a system of her own, perhaps working from left to right because that's the way she reads, or perhaps she has very sensibly decided to deal with the big numbers *before* the little numbers.

In some classrooms today children are being given opportunities to discover or devise their own computational procedures. In most classrooms, however, second graders are still being taught the procedures shown below for adding and subtracting large numbers:

Addition: Add 37 + 54.

Step 1:   Add the ones. Regroup (or carry).

$$\begin{array}{r} \overset{1}{} \\ 37 \\ + 54 \\ \hline 1 \end{array}$$

Step 2:   Add the tens, including the tens you regrouped.

$$
\begin{array}{r}
{}^{1} \\
37 \\
+\,54 \\
\hline
91
\end{array}
$$

Subtraction: Subtract 54 from 91.

Step 1:   Look at the ones. Regroup (borrow) if necessary.

$$
\begin{array}{r}
{}^{8\,11} \\
\cancel{91} \\
-\,54 \\
\hline

\end{array}
$$

Step 2:   Subtract the ones.

$$
\begin{array}{r}
{}^{8\,11} \\
\cancel{91} \\
-\,54 \\
\hline
7
\end{array}
$$

Step 3:   Subtract the tens.

$$
\begin{array}{r}
{}^{8\,11} \\
\cancel{91} \\
-\,54 \\
\hline
37
\end{array}
$$

If you or your child are confused about this procedure, see *Have More Time?* on page 147 for a way to show the method concretely. Sometimes you will approve of the methods used, sometimes you won't. These few guidelines will help smooth the way:

1. Try not to pass along your own anxiety about math. This may sound simple, but it's not. If your second grader is struggling, you may feel a strong urge to sympathize: "I always hated math, too. It must run in the family." Block that urge. Remember, your child will suffer from math anxiety only if you pass it along to her. By nature, many second graders are worriers. Your child needs to hear over and over again that you truly believe she can succeed.

2. Try not to tell your child how to solve a problem. Replace "Here, let me show you" with "How do you think you could solve that problem?" By approaching problems in this way, you encourage your child to stop and *think* about the problem before her. You also run less risk of teaching a method that will conflict with what she is learning at school.

3. Make sure your child has a good strong background in the number concepts behind the computation. To add and subtract larger numbers,

your child will need a thorough understanding of the base-ten place-value system. Many of the activities below reinforce that understanding. See also page 127.

4. Make sure you are familiar with the computation methods your child is learning at school. Talk with her teacher. Take a good look at her instructional materials. If possible, sit in on her class during math time. The more you know about what your child is doing in school, the easier it will be to support her at home.

5. Above all, keep it light. If math becomes a battlefield now, you will surely lose the war, and your child will learn to hate math. Show your child that math does not have to be threatening. Don't be afraid to take a few risks or make some walloping mistakes—that's half the fun of mathematics. And try, try, try to keep your sense of humor. There is no greater gift you can give your child.

Remember that addition and subtraction of larger numbers are *introduced* in second grade—usually late in the year, at that. Many children find these concepts to be tough, and most are not completely confortable with the skills until well into third or fourth grade. If you wish to show your child a different way to add or subtract larger numbers, check with her teacher first.

HAVE FIVE MINUTES?

➤ Use drinking straws and rubber bands to make bundles of tens. Set aside a pile of loose straws to serve as ones. Keep these handy to use as manipulatives when working out double-digit addition and subtraction problems.

➤ Talk out loud about how you figure out problems in your head. Say, "You know how I figured that out so fast? I thought, 49 is just one less than 50, so I added 50 instead of 49 and then just took one away." Let your child see you struggling with problems and coming at them from different angles. The point here is not to teach your child specific strategies but rather to teach her that there are lots of ways to get to a solution—some of which you haven't even thought of yet!

➤ Whenever possible, avoid giving a straight answer—For example:
"How old are you, Mom?"
"Well, I was born in 1961. How old does that make me?"

Some second graders delight in these kinds of problems and will look forward to turning the tables on you—"What do you want for dinner?" "What I want is flat and has cheese and tomato sauce on it." Others may place their hands firmly on their hips and tell you, "I'm serious!" Never fear. You'll find out very quickly which kind of second grader you have!

➤When reading a chapter book to your child, ask him how many more pages you have to go before you reach the end.

➤Do you have a long car ride ahead? Here's a tough one. Ask your child to find all the different combinations of two numbers that add up to 100 (1 + 99, 42 + 58, and so on). See what strategies your child comes up with to find the combinations.

➤If you are shopping in a drugstore or another place where there are small items for sale, give your child a dollar to spend on anything he wants. Chances are, he will amaze you with his addition and subtraction abilities!

➤Read *The Philharmonic Gets Dressed*, by Karla Kuskin (HarperCollins). The book, which follows 105 musicians as they get ready for a concert, is chock-full of charmingly candid photographs and chatty facts and figures—for example, "Forty-five men stand up to pull on their trousers, and forty-seven sit down." Use the information in the book to make up addition and subtraction problems for your child to solve: "Let's see. There are 92 men and 13 women. How many does that make all together?" Then ask your child to do the same. Ask your librarian to recommend other picture books that might lend themselves to talking about numbers and computation. Here are a few to get you started:
  • *The Boy Who Was Followed Home*, by Margaret Mahy (Dial)
  • *The King's Chessboard*, by David Birch (Dial)
  • *Komodo!* by Peter Sis (Clarion)
  • *Moira's Birthday*, by Robert Munsch (Annick Press)
  • *17 Kings and 42 Elephants*, by Margaret Mahy (Dial)

HAVE MORE TIME?

➤Since writing numbers is still a relatively new skill, many second graders have difficulty aligning the numbers in addition and subtraction problems in columns on the page. If your child has difficulty writing out a problem at home, suggest that he turn his paper so that the printed lines go up and down. The lines create ready-made columns for ones, tens, and hundreds, and keep those numbers in order.

➤Many board and card games provide excellent practice in multi-digit computation. If your child enjoys board games, try playing classic games like Monopoly or the game of Life. Yahtzee is superb for practicing addition, as is any card game like gin rummy, where the players keep a cumulative score. In addition, many of the games suggested in other sections—especially Number Sense, page 123, Place Value, page 127, and Addition and Subtraction Facts Through 18, page 133—can be easily adapted for addition and subtraction practice. See especially:

- Make a Number (page 129). Instead of making one number, players use the dice to generate numbers that they fill in on an addition or subtraction form. The player with the highest sum or difference wins.

$$+ \underline{\quad}\ \underline{\quad} \qquad\qquad - \underline{\quad}\ \underline{\quad}$$

- Hangmath (page 135). Change the form to include two- and three-digit numbers in the problem.

➤ If you feel that an alternative procedure for addition or subtraction might make pencil-and-paper computation easier for your child, you might want to try one of those listed below. Remember, before suggesting a different method to your child, check with the teacher.

Alternative Addition Methods

1. Add the numbers from left to right.

   $$\begin{array}{r} 245 \\ + 167 \\ \hline \end{array}$$

300	1. Add the hundreds.
+ 100	2. Add the tens.
12	3. Add the ones.
412	4. Add the hundreds, tens, and ones together.

2. Some children do just fine carrying their ones to the next column, but then forget that they are there when it comes to adding that column. Instead of carrying the number to the top of the problem, have your child try carrying it below the problem as shown.

   $$\begin{array}{r} {}^{1} \\ 65 \\ + 18 \\ \hline 83 \end{array} \qquad\qquad \begin{array}{r} 65 \\ + 18 \\ {}_{1}\overline{} \\ 83 \end{array}$$

3. If one number is close enough to a round number, you might suggest changing the numbers so that one is easier to add like this:

   $$\begin{array}{r} 49 \\ + 36 \\ \hline \end{array} \begin{array}{c} \rightarrow \text{ add 1} \rightarrow \\ \rightarrow \qquad \rightarrow \end{array} \begin{array}{r} 50 \\ + 36 \\ \hline 86 \end{array} \rightarrow \text{ subtract 1} \begin{array}{r} 49 \\ 36 \\ \hline 85 \end{array}$$

Alternative Subtraction Method

1. If one number is close enough to a round number, you might suggest changing the numbers so that one is easier to subtract:

```
  74   →          74              74
 –39   →  add 1  +40              39
 ____            ____            ____
                  34   →  add 1   35
```

Money

The ability to identify the names and values of coins and to add and subtract money is measured by questions 14, 15, and 16 in the Math Assessment.

Are you looking for a way to get your second grader more interested in math? You don't have to look any farther than your own pocket. Money—the great motivator!

Few children this age need to be pushed or prodded into learning about money. These are the entrepreneurial years—the years of lemonade stands and piggy banks and high-level negotiations on the subject of allowances. Even if your child still occasionally forgets that a quarter is worth twenty-five cents, she understands deep down inside that the more she knows about money, the better off she's going to be.

There is no better way to teach your child about money than to give her control over money of her own. If you haven't begun to give your child an allowance, now is the time to start. If you prefer instead to pay for household chores done, now's the time to negotiate the terms and make a list of fees. Handling money gives your child practice in estimation, place value, computation, and problem-solving skills. She will also get an idea of what the decimal system is all about. (You'll be grateful for this when she hits sixth grade.) Most important, she will know that she can understand and control her money—a kind of confidence many adults would be grateful to have!

HAVE FIVE MINUTES?

➤Whenever you give your child money for any reason, present her with a number of coins or bills and let her count out the appropriate amount. You'll find that even the most casual junior banker will snap to attention when the money she's counting is her own. As your child becomes more proficient with money, pay her in larger bills or coins and ask her to make change for you.

➤Encourage your child to dump her money out of her bank and count it—often. Whenever she wants to buy something from a store or catalog, ask, "How much money do you have? How much does this cost? About how much more do you think you need before you can buy this?"

➤Watch your child count change. You may assume that she will of course start counting with the larger coin values. Some children do this naturally; others do not. If she starts with the pennies, show her how much easier it is to start counting the big coins first.

➤Teach your child how to "count on" to make change. Suppose, for example, your child has given you four dimes for a 37¢ item. Count the change—37, 38, 39, 40—as you put three pennies into her hand.

➤While you're waiting for your order at a restaurant, empty your pocket or coin purse onto the table. Take turns coming up with different ways to sort the coins.

➤On vacation, during a shopping excursion, or on any special outing, give your child control over her own spending money. If you are planning to buy books for your child at the school book fair, for example, give her part of the money you expect to spend. Say, "Here is ten dollars. You can buy any books you'd like, as long as you don't spend more than this ten dollars."

➤Ask money questions like the following:
  • How many quarters are in a dollar? How many dimes? How many nickels?
  • If I have 17¢, what coins might I have?
  • I have 36 pennies. How many dimes can I get?
  • If I trade 9 pennies for 1 dime, am I getting a good deal?

HAVE MORE TIME?

➤Read *Alexander, Who Used to Be Rich Last Sunday,* by Judith Viorst (Macmillan). Give your child seven dimes, four nickels, and ten pennies. As you read the story, have your child give you the coins that Alexander spends or loses, and ask her to tell you how much is left by the end of the book.

➤Give your child a store circular or catalog and an amount to "spend"—say, 99¢ or $100. Have your child circle the items she thinks she could buy if she had that amount of money. Have her check her estimates by counting out the cost of each item with play money.

➤ How much change is at the bottom of your junk drawer, your glove compartment, or your purse? Have your child guess, search the drawer for change, and count up the total. You might agree to deposit the amount in her bank account or pay her a certain percentage—say ten cents per dollar—for her efforts.

➤ This is an age when the entrepreneurial spirit runs high, but skill and perseverance sometimes lag behind. Here are some easy-to-execute ideas for your young tycoon:

- Lemonade stands are a perennial favorite, but don't forget that the public gets hungry as well as thirsty. Help your child make popcorn, package it in small and large plastic bags, and price it accordingly.
- Just how many old party favors and McDonald's Happy Meal toys can fit in one child's desk drawer? Your second grader may feel better about parting with some of these treasures if she sells them at a toy sale in her front yard. Encourage her to price them to sell!
- Second graders are still too little to take on some of the classic kid jobs, like mowing lawns, baby-sitting, and shoveling sidewalks. But your child might be able to perform smaller services for pay. How about picking up debris after a storm, watering the window boxes, or taking in your neighbors' mail while they are away for the weekend? The pay does not need to be great. It's the pride of earning an honest dollar, or dime, that counts.
- For more moneymaking ideas, read *Making Cents, Every Kid's Guide to Money* (Little, Brown). Although most of the ideas in the book are for older kids, many can be scaled down to meet your junior entrepreneur's needs.

➤ Read "Smart," from *Where the Sidewalk Ends*, by Shel Silverstein (HarperCollins). Second graders love to figure out why the boy in the poem keeps making such bad deals. Here are some other good books about money:

- *Arthur's Funny Money*, by Lillian Hoban (HarperCollins)
- *If You Made a Million*, by David M. Schwartz (Scholastic)
- *Irene and the Big Fine Nickel*, by Irene Smalls-Hector (Little, Brown)
- *Lemonade Parade*, by Ben Brooks (Kids Can Press)
- *The Purse*, by Kathy Caple (Houghton Mifflin)
- *Summer Business*, by Charles Martin (HarperCollins)

Time

The ability to tell time to the hour, half hour, quarter hour, and five minutes is measured by questions 17 and 18 in the Math Assessment.

You tell your second grader that dinner will be ready in an hour, and he comes back to the kitchen in five minutes. At the computer, your child pleads for "just two more minutes" to conquer the world, and you see that he has twenty-six more countries to go. At two o'clock in the afternoon, your child asks, "Did I already have breakfast today?" You think he should have more of a sense of time by now.

Ask any parents of a fourth or fifth grader when their child learned to tell time, and chances are they will say, "I don't know—sometime around second grade." Although many first graders can recognize the hour and half hour, most children do not have a firm understanding of linear time until they're well into the second or even third grade, when something suddenly clicks.

Although your child can probably read a digital clock by now, don't be fooled into thinking that he knows how to tell time to the minute. The concept of time is difficult, even for adults: Your flight leaves at 21:40. What time do you need to leave for the airport? It will take many, many experiences with analog clocks for your child to develop strong time-telling skills and a good sense of time. And even then, chances are you'll still find yourself saying, "When I say now, I mean *now*."

HAVE FIVE MINUTES?

➤ Make sure that your child has an *analog* (not digital) clock in his bedroom, in the kitchen, and wherever else he is likely to need to check the time. Refer to the clock often and show him how to read it: "Let's see, the big hand is on the three, so that means it's fifteen minutes past eight." If your child knows how to tell time by the hour and half hour, have him tell you the times, using those terms: "It's just before two o'clock. It's almost four-thirty."

➤ If you can afford it, buy your child a wristwatch of his own. Most second graders adore their watches. Chances are, your child's watch will become one of his most prized possessions. He will wear it with pride, check it every five minutes, and learn a great deal about time when you aren't even around!

➤ Teach your child the vocabulary of time and use it often. Try to remember to refer to the big hand as the "minute hand" and to the little hand as the "hour hand." Use the terms "quarter to," "quarter after," and "half past" as well as "one-forty," "forty minutes after one," and "twenty minutes before two."

➤ Ask your child to name some things he can do in two minutes. Then time him.

➤ Whenever a job needs to be done, challenge your child to race the clock: "I bet you can't get dressed by quarter after eight," or "Let's see if we can empty the dishwasher by quarter to six."

➤ To give your child a way to visualize a *half hour* and *a quarter hour,* draw clock faces on a piece of plain paper. Have your child color in the appropriate fraction of a circle.

➤ Don't forget that calendars also mark time. Hang a calendar in your child's bedroom, or help him make one on the computer. Just before bedtime, help him record one special thing about the day on the calendar. Talk about the day's date—"Today is Monday, October 17"—and refer to other events by date: "When did your last tooth fall out? Can you find the date?"

HAVE MORE TIME?

➤ If your child does not have a toy clock with movable hands, help him make one out of a paper plate, a brad fastener, and construction paper. Have him use the clock to show you the answers to word problems like these: "You get on the schoolbus at 7:45. It takes you fifteen minutes to get to school. What time do you usually get to school?" and "It takes two hours to get to Aunt Mimi's house. If we leave at 2:30, what time will we get there?"

➤ Read *The Scarecrow Clock* by George Mendoxa (Holt). Suggest that your child pretend to be the scarecrow and use his arms to represent the hour and minute hands on a clock. Have him position his arms to show a time for you to guess. Then switch roles and see if he can guess the time you demonstrate.

➤ Read *Clocks and More Clocks* by Pat Hutchins (Macmillan), and then have your child check the clocks in your house to see if they are all synchronized.

Measurement

The ability to measure objects using nonstandard and standard units of measurement is measured by questions 19 and 20 in the Math Assessment.

Follow your second grader's movements as she gets ready for school. How much orange juice will fill her glass for breakfast? Do last year's pants still fit, or are they too short? Will all those books *and* her favorite stuffed animal fit in her backpack? How cold is it outside? Does she need a coat? It's not even eight o'clock, and your child is already measuring.

When adults think of measurements, they usually think of inches and feet or pounds and ounces or cups and gallons. Children, on the other hand, begin by comparing ("Which piece of cake do I want?") and estimating ("When should I stop pouring?"). Eventually they move on to measuring with nonstandard units. ("The bathroom is twelve steps away from my bedroom"), and finally they learn to use standard units ("I weigh 62 pounds"). Each of these measuring techniques has advantages and disadvantages. Knowing the distance to the bathroom in centimeters probably won't help your child decide if she can get there in time, and (at least nowadays) few people need to know their weight in salt.

It is highly likely that your child will do more work with standard units, such as inches or centimeters, this year than she has done in the past. However, she should still spend a great deal of time estimating and comparing size, weight, and volume, and measuring with nonstandard units. Only through these experiences will your child gain the measurement sense she needs in order to use standard units effectively.

Most school systems now require children to learn both metric and U.S. customary measures. Check with your child's teacher to find out if your child's program stresses one system over another. Do *not* attempt to teach your second grader how to convert from one system to the other.

HAVE FIVE MINUTES?

➤ Estimate and measure. How many hands, one over the other, does it take to get to the end of a baseball bat? How many child lengths long is the bedroom? How many chocolate chips will fit in a muffin cup? Got an important phone call to make? Send your second grader off to measure the width of the driveway in paper clips.

➤ Ask, "What could you use to measure the length of a caterpillar? A fish? A cow? A whale?"

➤ Ask these questions:
  • "Do you think this suitcase is heavier than you are? How can we find out?"
  • "If there were a fire in our house, which would be the closest way out from your bedroom, the front door or the back door? How can we find out?"
  • "We need 20 ounces of tomato sauce. Should we get the large can or the small can? How can we tell?"

➤ If you are trying to get your taxes done and your child is not being much help, send her off on a measuring scavenger hunt. Have her find
  • Ten things that are shorter than your calculator
  • Five things that weigh more than your tax file
  • Three things that hold less liquid than your coffee cup

➤ When your child is taking a linear measurement, show her how to line up the measuring tool properly. Demonstrate how to begin measuring from a baseline. If she measures the length of the counter, for example, she must begin at one end and not in the middle. Failure to begin at the baseline accounts for most measuring errors in the early elementary grades.

➤ Using the standard measures your child is learning, ask questions like the following:
  • "What would be a good thing to measure in inches?"
  • "Would you use centimeters or meters to measure the height of a daffodil? How about a tree?"

HAVE MORE TIME?

➤ Give your child as many opportunities to measure as possible. Carpentry and sewing provide practical reasons for measuring. Because a second grader's knowledge of fractions is shaky at best, try to find activities in which your child can measure to whole numbers. Help your second grader come up with a design—keeping it simple will be the hard part—and then show her how to measure twice, cut once.

➤ Invite your child to cook with you. Even if you are not following a recipe with specific measures, have a cup, measuring spoons, and a ruler handy. Ask your child to measure out a cup of macaroni, to snap the beans into one-inch pieces, or to scoop out a tablespoon of honey. If you are really adventuresome, give her some ingredients—cereal, nuts, raisins, and chocolate chips are good starters—and have her come up with a recipe for her own snack.

➤ Help your child rearrange the furniture in her room. Have her estimate whether or not the furniture will fit in various positions. Will the desk fit between the bed and the window? Then have her use lengths of string to compare the length of the furniture and the length of the opening to check her estimates.

➤ Have your child make a book about herself. Although most parents keep close track of every pound gained and inch grown during their child's first couple of years, enthusiasm for record keeping falls off as the child gets older. Shift the responsibility for measuring to your child. Give her a small notebook and a tape measure, string, ruler, measuring cups, scales, or other measuring tools. Have her draw a picture of herself and record her height and weight and the measurements of various body parts. See if she can come up with her own method for taking difficult measures like the circumference of her head. On other pages, your child can list other timely measurements, such as

- How far she can broad-jump
- How much sand fits in one of her shoes
- How much rice she can hold in one hand
- How heavy a pile of books she can lift
- How much she weighs when she's holding her cat.
  And don't forget how many teeth she's currently missing!

➤ Picture books about measuring range from the factual to the fantastic. Here are a few surefire hits for second graders:

- *The Biggest, Smallest, Fastest, Tallest Things You've Ever Heard Of,* by Robert Lopshire (Crowell)
- *Chicken Soup with Rice,* by Maurice Sendak (HarperCollins)
- "The Crow and the Pitcher" and other stories in *Fairy Tales and Fables,* by Gyo Fujikawa (Putnam)
- *The Dinosaur Who Lived in My Backyard,* by B. G. Hennessy (Viking)
- *8,000 Stones: A Chinese Folktale,* by Diane Wolkstein (Doubleday)
- *How Big Is a Foot?,* by Rolf Myller (Antheneum)

Fractions

The ability to recognize equal parts and identify fractions is measured by questions 21, 22, and 23 in the Math Assessment.

Children know a lot about fractions even before they get to school. Any child over the age of two knows what half a cookie is, and a seven-year-old has no problem dividing a bag of M&Ms among three people. Yet by the time they are in sixth grade, most children have become so befuddled by fractions that many give up trying to understand them.

What happens? In the past, school programs have avoided teaching fractions in the early years, preferring to have children work exclusively with whole numbers. Learning how to add and subtract whole numbers is hard enough, the reasoning goes, so let's leave fractions for later on. Unfortunately whole numbers and fractions do not behave at all alike. (Why is four bigger than two, but ¼ is smaller than ½?)

Luckily, the best mathematics programs now include lots of hands-on work with fractions as a natural extension of what children already know about the world around them. Through concrete experiences, children build on their informal knowledge (remember that cookie?) so that even as they get into working with models (a circle cut into two equal pieces) or symbols (½), fractions continue to make sense.

Your child needs to understand three simple but vital concepts about fractions:

1. Fractions name numbers of *equal parts*—that is, there is no such thing as the big half and the little half.
2. In a fraction, the bottom number tells the number of equal parts and the top number tells how many of those parts have been chosen.
3. A fraction can name part of an area (as in ⅙ of a pizza) or part of a set (as in ⅔ of the children are girls).

Drilling your second grader with flash cards will do little to help him build this basic understanding. Instead, help him gain fraction sense by giving him lots of opportunities to see how fractional parts and wholes work together.

HAVE FIVE MINUTES?

➤ Young children seem to know instinctively that fractions are used when whole numbers don't work, whereas older kids seem to think fractions were invented to make life complicated. Keep your youngster's pro-fraction spirit alive by pointing out times when fractions come in handy. How else could you divide one container of ice cream equally among four people? Notice fraction notations that you come across in the sports section of the newspaper or while shopping for groceries. Talk about what each fraction is part of: what's the whole, or *one?* Half an inch is a lot different from half a mile. Half of my little apple may not satisfy my hunger as well as half of your big one.

➤After you have cut brownies, pie, or lasagna into equal portions, have your child count the number of equal parts and then tell you what fraction of the whole his piece is—say, 1 out of 8, or ⅛. Ask questions like these:

- "If you were really hungry would you rather have ⅛ or ¼ of this pan of brownies?"
- "If there were ten people here instead of eight, how should I have cut this lasagna?"
- "If I had cut this pie into thirds, how many pieces would there have been?"

➤Play I Spy using fractions: "I spy with my little eye something that is almost half blue" (a blue-striped shirt).

➤When you are waiting in line, ask, "How many people are standing in this line? What fraction of people in this line are wearing glasses?"

HAVE MORE TIME?

➤Second graders love to arrange things. Have your child sort his stuffed animals, action figures, or coin collection to demonstrate various fractions. For example, you might ask him to arrange his animals so that half are alike. Leave it up to him to decide how to sort the animals. He may decide to arrange them so that half are striped, half are mammals, or half are his very favorite stuffed animals in the whole wide world.

➤Give your child a piece of graph paper and a set of markers. Have him make a design by coloring in squares of different colors. Give him challenges such as "Make one half one color and the other half another color."

➤Read the book *Eating Fractions* by Bruce McMillan. After you've had a chance to pore over the mouth-watering photos, invite your second grader to help you create your own fraction feast!

➤On a rainy Saturday, suggest that your child set up a pizza parlor. Give him white paper plates, markers, glue, and colored construction paper. To make pizzas, he can color the plates red and cut mushrooms, pepperoni, or other toppings out of construction paper according to the specific order. Place orders such as "I'd like half mushroom and half broccoli, please." Have your child make up a price list, and don't forget to count your change!

Geometry

The ability to recognize shapes is measured by questions 24, 25, and 26 in the Math Assessment.

Think back to when your second grader was a preschooler making a tower with blocks. Already she seemed to know so much about shapes. She knew which blocks were the same and which were different, which would roll and which wouldn't, which would balance and which would make the whole tower come tumbling down. At her kindergarten assessment, she was probably asked to name a circle, a square, and a triangle. And chances are, these shape names—if not a few others as well—are second nature to her now.

So why continue to teach second graders about shapes? Geometry is more than memorizing the names of shapes. Learning about shapes and space and how they relate to each other helps children develop all sorts of problem-solving skills—classification and visualization, for example—that are essential to both mathematics and everyday life. How often have you heard someone say, "I just can't visualize it"? Every time you try to follow a map, understand a diagram, or buy a rug for your living room, you use your powers of spatial thinking. Help your child develop those powers by giving her lots of opportunities to play with shapes and patterns.

For other activities involving patterns, see page 72.

HAVE FIVE MINUTES?

➤ Talk about shapes that you see around you. What shape is that pine tree or the tunnel at the playground? Is that window a square or a rectangle? While you are standing in line at the bank or sitting in the doctor's waiting room, challenge your child to a shape hunt. Choose a shape, such as circle or square, and see how many you can find in your immediate surroundings.

For inspiration, check out *Circles, Triangles and Squares*, by Tana Hoban (Macmillan) or *Listen to a Shape*, by Marcia Brown (Franklin Watts). Both books contain beautiful photographs filled with everyday shapes.

➤ Use your finger to draw a shape on your child's back and have her identify it. Then switch roles.

➤ Get into the habit of using maps. You can find city and transit maps in most libraries, and many telephone books include maps of the local area. If you've been thinking about investing in a wall map, atlas, or globe, now's a good time to do it. Refer to maps often. Show your second grader the route to school or to her best friend's house. Find the state where Uncle Charlie lives. When you read that the zoo just got a new Siberian tiger, point out its native habitat on the globe.

➤ Look for symmetry in your surroundings. Children who are used to looking for symmetry have an easier time recognizing shapes of equal size and the equal parts of fractions. When you're waiting for the school bus, look around. Can you find something that is symmetrical? How about that fern leaf? The duplex across the street? What about your child's own body?

➤ At a restaurant, invite your child to use toothpicks, sugar packets, or cutlery to construct and name as many different shapes as she can. If she runs out of shapes and the food still hasn't come, challenge her to use the toothpicks to make a maze from the salt to the pepper shaker.

➤ If your food *still* hasn't come, write large capital letters on your child's napkin or place mat. Have your child place her knife in the middle of the letter and look at each side's reflection to see if it is symmetrical or not. Use letters with vertical symmetry first (A, H, M, and so on), then try to trick her by throwing in one with horizontal symmetry (B, C, D, and so on).

HAVE MORE TIME?

➤ If your child's wooden blocks have been languishing in the back of her closet, get them out. Or help her create a new construction kit out of cardboard boxes and other reusable items. You may find that your second grader will prefer to make space stations or pony corrals rather than the castles of her preschool years, but that's fine. Use the vocabulary of geometry as you talk about her creations: "Oh, that cylinder makes a great air traffic control center," or "How many blocks did you use to build the perimeter of the corral?" You will find that the words will slip painlessly into her everyday vocabulary.

➤ Make a tangram—a Chinese puzzle made up of geometric shapes. Use the pattern below to draw the puzzle on a piece of poster board. Have your child cut out the pieces. Can she put them back together to make a square? What other shapes and pictures can she make with the pieces? Make two sets and take turns creating and copying each other's designs.

Wooden and plastic tangrams are available in many toy and educational supply stores. You can also find books of tangram pictures and puzzles in libraries and bookstores, but your child may prefer to create a tangram book of her own!

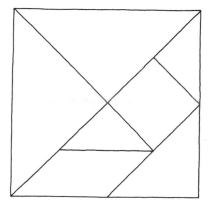

➤Make snowflakes. Have your child predict what shape each cut will make.

➤Give your child a collection of reusable materials such as plastic tubs, cardboard tubes, bottle caps, and rubber bands. Challenge her to make an action contraption that can roll. Prop a board or large book up at one end so that she can test her contraption's action and adjust the design accordingly.

➤The art of origami, or paper folding, reinforces all sorts of geometric concepts. Most second graders can make simple origami figures, and they love the sense of accomplishment they feel when they come up with a finished design. Books of simple designs for children are available in libraries and bookstores.

➤At an art museum or in a book of paintings at the library, notice how artists use shapes, symmetry, and tessellation (mosaic) in their work. Look for the works of artists such as M. C. Escher, Pict Mondrian, Henri Matisse, Paul Klee, and Alexander Calder. At home, invite your child to use paints or shapes cut from construction paper to create geometric artwork of her own.

The book *Shapes,* by Paul Yenawine (Museum of Modern Art, Delacorte) shows how shapes contribute to different works of art in New York's Museum of Modern Art.

Problem Solving

The ability to solve word problems is measured by questions 27, 28, and 29 in the Math Assessment.

You remember word problems: those dreaded pages in your math book filled with stories about apples and oranges and trains traveling toward each other at a certain speed in the middle of the night. The page was usually labeled "Show What You Know" or some such title, but just the prospect of facing a word problem could make you forget that 2 + 2 = 4.

Luckily, times have changed. In most classrooms today the teaching of computation and mathematical concepts *begins* rather than ends with problem-solving. A good program assumes that young children learn math best through concrete, physical experiences with problem-solving. This is nothing new—it's how your child has learned to solve problems at home.

Problem-solving situations at home pop up all the time. Every time your child helps you put the groceries away or counts the money in her piggy bank or tries to wrap a present for a friend's birthday, she is building her problem-solving skills. The strategies she uses to solve these problems are the same ones you use when you plan a dinner, balance your checkbook, or retile the kitchen floor. These are tools your child will use throughout her life.

How, then, can you help your second grader develop good problem-solving skills? Here are some suggestions.

Approach problems with a determined spirit.

Instead of ripping up the instruction manual to the VCR in frustration, take a deep breath and announce, "Okay, I'm going to figure this out if it's the last thing I do!" Talk through your problem-solving strategy, even if it's kicking the stupid machine ("It worked last time"). Let your child see you making mistakes and trying different approaches to the same problem. ("Well, I followed the directions and nothing happened. Maybe I should look at the diagram.") Keep in mind how you would like your child to approach life's little—and big—difficulties. Do you want him to be flexible or to freeze? To snarl in frustration or to keep his sense of humor? To hang in there or to give up after a few unsuccessful tries?

Don't rescue your child.

This may sound harsh, but the most important lesson your second grader can learn is that he can solve problems on his own. Be patient, and watch your child come up with solutions on his own. Instead of saying, "Here's how you do it," ask, "How do you think you can solve this problem?" or "What might help you figure this out?"

If your child is struggling with a problem, suggest that he try one of the following strategies.

You may want to try them yourself!

- use objects
- act it out
- draw a picture
- make an organized list
- look for a pattern
- guess and check

HAVE FIVE MINUTES?

➤ Whenever possible, state your parental concerns as problems to be solved. Instead of shouting "The school bus will be here in five minutes. Put your shoes on right now!" try turning the situation into a problem to solve: "It's five minutes to eight. The bus will be here at eight. How long do you have to put your shoes on and brush your teeth?"

➤ Point out patterns you hear or see in your surroundings: "Look at that row of cars in the parking lot. Two red, one white, two red, one white!" Ask what should come next in the pattern. At odd moments, give your child a pattern like the ones below. Ask him to show or tell you what comes next in the pattern.
  - Touch your nose, touch your chin, touch your head, touch your nose . . .
  - Say, "Beep, beep, honk, honk, beep, beep, honk, honk . . ."
  - Arrange in a pattern: toothpicks | / \ | / \ | / \ . . .
  - Draw a pattern with your finger on your child's back: x x o o o x x o o o . . .

➤ Encourage your child to come up with multiple solutions to a problem: "What are some other ways you could get to school if you missed the bus and if I couldn't take you there?"

➤ Make up brain teasers—for example, "I'm thinking of someone in this family. The person has brown eyes but doesn't wear glasses. Who is it?"

➤ At a restaurant, a ball game, or any other place where there is a list of prices, numbers, or statistics, give your child an answer and ask him to make up the question. For example, at the post office you might say, "The answer is 34¢. What could the question be?" One possible question: "If you bought a 32¢ stamp and a 2¢ stamp, how much would it cost?"

➤Ask, "What are some things that you can do with an empty yogurt container (or egg carton or cereal box)? Let's see how many things we can list."

➤On a walk, notice the numbers on houses you pass, and look for a pattern. Have your child predict what the number on the next house will be.

HAVE MORE TIME?

➤Find opportunities for your child to collect and analyze data. Most second graders would make great Gallup or Nielsen employees—their enthusiasm for taking surveys knows no bounds. Send your child off on a data-collecting spree. Have him ask these questions of family members or friends at school: What is your favorite color (or ice cream or sports team or bug)? What year were you born? Who do you think is going to win the Super Bowl? How many teeth have you lost? How many hours of television did you watch yesterday? Help your child organize the information into a list or on a graph. Discuss his findings, and use a copy machine or computer to print up the results for the participants of the survey.

➤Play games of strategy. Second grade is not too early to begin learning the moves of chess. Though your child probably won't be challenging IBM's Big Blue this year, just practicing the moves is great training in memory and logic. Here are some other games that enhance strategic thinking:
Battleship
Checkers
Dominoes
Mancala (see page 137)
Parcheesi
Solitaire

If you have the time and patience, you can make a homemade version of each of these games. Also, look for books of children's games in your library or bookstore. Many of the games in *Kids' Games* by Phil Wiswell (Doubleday) and *The Book of Classic Board Games* (Klutz) are appropriate now and will take your child well into high school.

➤Second graders are big thinkers. Let your child plan and execute a project *by himself* from start to finish. You'd be surprised at how many problem-solving skills a second grader uses while making a breakfast of yogurt and English muffins for the entire family. Here are some other ideas that might appeal to your second grader:
• Taking charge of a holiday celebration—for example, putting

together a Halloween costume, planning a birthday party, or preparing a Fourth of July picnic
- Building a fort
- Planning and planting a garden
- Making an obstacle course or a miniature golf course
- Putting on a play, a puppet show, or a magic show
- Making a board game

➤Introduce your child to Venn diagrams. Draw two interlocking rings on a large piece of paper, or make the rings out of string or yarn. On slips of paper, label the rings Things Made of Metal, Things Made of Plastic. Label the overlapping section Things Made of Metal and Plastic. Dump out the junk drawer, have your child sort its contents into the three groups, and place each object where it belongs on the Venn diagram.

Multiplication and Division Readiness

The ability to create equal groups and divide a collection is measured by question 30 in the Math Assessment.

Many second graders are eager to learn how to multiply. They know that multiplication is the next step beyond addition and subtraction, and they feel sure they are ready to take it. You might even hear your own second grader boast, "Oh, I already know how to multiply. It's easy!" Hearing all this enthusiasm, you might be tempted to start teaching your child the multiplication facts—why not strike while the iron's hot? There are a couple of good reasons why you shouldn't bring out the flash cards quite yet.

First of all, your child already knows a lot about multiplication and division (2 groups of 3 crackers, *of course*, make 6 crackers, and 6 crackers divided between 2 people, *of course*, means 3 crackers apiece). Rote memorization of tables or procedures will not build upon this great intuitive knowledge.

Second, as impressive as it is to hear a second grader rattle off her multiplication tables, memorization can go only so far. Multiplication and division procedures are going to get more complex. Your child needs to understand *at the very minimum* that multiplication means putting groups together and that division means splitting one group into other equal groups. Young children gain that type of understanding only through hands-on experience with objects.

Many second grade programs don't approach multiplication and division readiness until the end of the year. Some don't approach it at all. By using the language of multiplication and division as you and your child combine or divide groups of objects, you can help your child get ready for these concepts when the time comes.

HAVE FIVE MINUTES?

➤ In a line or a roomful of people, ask "How many feet are in this room?" Ask your second grader to estimate first and then skip-count by twos to find out.

➤ Teach your child how to use tally marks to make groups of five. How many cups of lemonade did he sell? How many points did he earn in that game of darts? How many people with Reebok sneakers will pass before you are called to board the airplane? Have your child skip-count by fives to find the total of the tallies.

cups sold ~~HHT~~ ll

➤ Whenever you are scoring points—in a ring toss or badminton game, for example—up the ante by making each point worth 2 or 3 or 5. Suggest that your child skip-count to figure out the score.

HAVE MORE TIME?

➤ If your child's room is about to be declared a national disaster area, try a new system for cleaning up. Say, "I wonder how many groups of five [or two or three or ten] you can make out of all the stuff on your floor." Suggest that your child try to sort the items as she makes her groups, so that she has a stack of five books, a pile of five dirty socks, a group of five play-

MATH
EXERCISES

167

ing pieces from assorted games, and so on. After she has made her groups, say, "Wow! You made six groups of five! Let's figure out how many that makes all together: five, ten, fifteen, twenty . . . Holy cow! That's thirty different things! No wonder we couldn't see your floor!"

➤ Is this a familiar picture? Your child is bugging you to play Star Wars or ponies, or whatever her current collectible toy passion is. You know that you should delight in the fantasy, but you are *really* tired of Star Wars. Try slipping a multiplication or division story into your play: "Oh-oh! Each escape pod holds only two people! How many pods are we going to need to save all eight of us?"

➤ Notice the illustrations in picture books you are reading aloud. After you have finished reading, go back and ask your child to count items like the buttons on *The Button Blanket* by Nan McNutt or the cats in *Millions of Cats* by Wanda Gag. Suggest skip-counting as an easier way to count. The following picture books are particularly well suited to skip counting:
- *The 500 Hats of Bartholomew Cubbins,* by Dr. Seuss (Vanguard Press). Sir Alaric, keeper of the King's Records, counts the hats in groups of five.
- *The King's Commissioners,* by Aileen Friedman (Scholastic)
- *Sea Squares,* by Joy Hulme (Hyperion)
- *Two, Four, Six, Eight: A Book About Legs,* by Ethel and Leonard Kessler (Dodd, Mead)
- *What Comes in 2's, 3's, 4's?,* by Suzanne Aker (Simon & Schuster)
- *Arctic Fives Arrive,* by Elinor Pinczes (Houghton Mifflin)

Math Enrichment

Like the child who seems to wake up one morning and begin to read at the age of four, some children seem to be born with the ability to think mathematically. For these children math just makes sense—it seems like a great way to organize the world. If your child is adding sales slips in her head while her classmates are working on addition facts to 18, you may be wondering if perhaps she shouldn't be getting *more*. The question is, more of what? If she knows addition and subtraction, shouldn't she be learning multiplication and division? If not, won't she be bored? If you don't move her ahead, won't you be holding her back?

The answer is, don't push her ahead, but don't hold her back. You want to broaden and deepen your second grader's understanding and experience. The fact that your second grader can perform the subtraction computation being taught in class doesn't necessarily mean that you should be drilling her on multiplication. But if she is trying to figure out how many cookies to bring to the table so that each person can have two, why not explore a little multiplication? Most children who catch on to math quickly do so because they are good at making generalizations. If you show a child that $3 + 3 + 3$ equals 3×3, she will probably generalize the rule to 4×4, 5×5, and so on.

To the casual observer, primary mathematics seems to be all about computation. Yet research has shown that many children with fine computation skills still have difficulty using those skills to solve problems. The ability to reason, think logically, and estimate must be strengthened and developed if your child is to continue to succeed in mathematics. In fact, if you prepare your child to become a confident, effective problem-solver, you will be doing more for her mathematical achievement than all the drills in the world. The task isn't as difficult as it sounds. Give your child a variety of problems—particularly problems involving concrete objects—and she will build her own understanding.

Enriching your child's study of math at home is easy. Problems in measurement, logic, and computation pop up all over the place:

- "Do we have time to stop by the library before your soccer game?"
- "The library is closed two days a week. What are the chances it's closed today?"
- "Each of the three of you took five books out of the library last time. How many books do we need to collect to take back?"

The best school programs are modeled after the way math presents itself in real life: *Here's the problem. Now, how are you going to solve it?* If your child is in this kind of program, she's getting lots of opportunities to work on problem-solving skills and mathematical reasoning, even if the computation itself is less than challenging.

However, if your child could almost do your taxes for you and yet continues to come home with pages full of addition problems, it's time to talk with her teacher. Even if the teacher is unwilling to let go of the textbook approach to mathematics, you may be able to come to an agreement about parallel assignments that will deepen and broaden your child's understanding. Perhaps your child can write her own story problems using some of the numbers on the workbook page. Or perhaps she can create addition puzzles for other children to solve. Either alternative would give your second grader a chance to build some mathematical reasoning skills as she practices the required computation. As you work with your child's teacher, try to keep several points in mind.

First of all, some children—particularly those with strong visual memories—find math facts and computation methods very easy to memorize. Unfortunately, this does not necessarily mean that they understand the process behind those mathematical tricks. To build a good foundation for the math challenges that lie ahead—multiplication, fractions, algebra, calculus—it is essential that every second grader continue to have lots practice with concrete objects.

Also remember that children who have a gift for math often come up with their own computation strategies before they are taught the standard procedures in school. When asked how she got an answer, many times such a child will simply say, "I thought about it," or "I figured it out." If your child is already comfortably using a strategy of her own and her teacher insists that she practice a different strategy, remind yourself and your child that looking at solving problems from different angles is a useful learning practice. The school-sanctioned strategy may not get your child to the answer any faster, but being exposed to it may help broaden her understanding of number theory and the computation process.

A third point to keep in mind is that, in trying to come up with a program that meets your child's needs, you must do your best to avoid any solution that isolates your child. A common proposal for individualizing curriculum is to have students work at their own pace in their textbooks. This arrangement is faulty, if not detrimental, for a number of reasons. For one thing, it focuses on getting the right answer to finish the page rather than on the *process* of solving a problem. It also ignores important by-products of instruction such as learning to follow classroom routines, learning to work within a group, and learning to communicate ideas. Furthermore, it ignores the fact that second graders are social creatures, that children learn best when they are active and involved with other people, and that children of this age generally process their learning by talking about it. Therefore, this kind of program makes it impossible for children to be stimulated by and to learn from each other.

Finally, no matter how superb your child's school math program is, her attitude toward math and her confidence in her ability will ultimately come directly from you. Just as a good reader still needs to be read to, a good math student still needs lots of opportunities to "do math" with the most important person in her life—you.

HAVE FIVE MINUTES?

➤ Give your child number patterns to solve. Provide the first four numbers in the sequence, and ask him to give you the next three:
18, 16, 14, 12, ___, ___, ___
22, 33, 44, 55, ___, ___, ___
1000, 1100, 1200, 1300, ___, ___, ___

➤ Point out the language of probability that you use every day. Notice the times either of you says phrases like *chances are, most likely, probably not, odds are, no doubt,* and *don't hold your breath!* Talk about your thinking behind the phrases. Why did your child say *"Probably not"* when you told him that perhaps he could have ten of his best friends over for a sleepover?

➤ Show your child how to find his lucky number:
  1. Write down your birth date in numbers—for example, 6-22-1990.
  2. Add the numbers together: $6 + 2 + 2 + 1 + 9 + 9 + 0 = 29$
  3. Add those digits together: $2 + 9 = 11$

4. Repeat until you get a one digit number: 1 + 1 = 2
5. The lucky number is 2!

➤Talk about possible combinations: "We've got two different kinds of cheese for appetizers and two different kinds of crackers. How many different combinations can we make with those ingredients?"

➤Have your child look for big, big numbers in old newspapers and magazines. Have him cut out the numbers and glue them onto sticky tags. Help him stick the tags in order from least to greatest along one wall of his room. As he finds new numbers, he can rearrange the tags accordingly until his row of numbers stretches around the perimeter of his room.

➤Talk about funny logic: "If the sun is shining, it isn't raining. The sun isn't shining, so it must be raining. What's wrong with this logic?"

➤Estimate, estimate. Compare your estimates and talk about how you came to them. (You may learn something.) Whenever possible, find a way to check your guesses. (Surprise!) Ask "Which would take longer, waiting for food in this restaurant or waiting for your turn in a game of Scrabble with Mom?"

➤Use the Roman numerals that you find in chapter books to introduce the Roman numeral system to your second grader. Check out other numeral systems such as the Egyptian numeral system shown below, and if your second grader seems particularly interested, have him design a numeral system of his own.

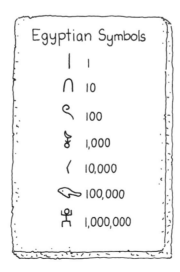

Egyptian Symbols

| | 1
∩ | 10
ς | 100
⚡ | 1,000
(| 10,000
◡ | 100,000
🧍 | 1,000,000

➤ Want a few peaceful moments with the Sunday papers? Give your child the coupon section. Tell him that if he clips coupons for things you need (emphasis on *need*) and keeps track of how much you save when you use them, he can keep the money saved.

➤ Whenever you run up against one of life's little difficulties, ask your child, "What do we need to know?" For example, "I'm not sure whether we should shop for school supplies at Save-a-Buck or SuperMart. What do we need to know?" or "Can we bake cookies this afternoon? What do we need to know?" Be aware, however, that this problem-solving approach can be turned back on you. If you say, for instance, "I don't know if we can go out for ice cream tonight or not. We'll see," your child may respond with "Well, Dad, what do you need to know?"

➤ Whenever your second grade math whiz is about to give up, remind him of what Albert Einstein once said, "Do not worry about your difficulties in mathematics; I can assure you that mine are still greater."

HAVE MORE TIME?

➤ Hide a coin or a small toy in your yard or home. Make a simple map of the yard or of the room where the treasure is hidden. Have your child follow the map to find the treasure. Then switch roles, and have your child draw a map for you.

➤ Elapsed time is a hard concept to grasp, even for a second grader who is comfortable with math. Give your child a stopwatch. It will become a prized possession, and every time he times something the watch will teach him just a little bit about elapsed time.

As a special activity, ask your second grader to estimate how many times he can hop in one minute and then time himself. After he has done this a few times with different exercises (jumping jacks, toe touches, sprints), reverse the activity by having him predict how long it will take him to hop twenty-five times.

➤ Play with probability. Make a copy of the 0–99 chart on page 191 in the back of the book. Have your child drop a penny from waist height onto the chart twenty times and record the numbers it lands on. Did it land on more numbers between 0 and 49 or between 50 and 99? Have him drop twenty more pennies. Did the results change? Repeat the experiment with different ranges of numbers—say, 0 to 74 and 75 to 100. Did the results change? Why?

➤ Teach your child to play poker. He'll love it.

➤ If you are looking for a gift for your second grader, think about investing in a children's atlas. Teach him how to use coordinates to find locations in the atlas (exactly where *is* Uzbekistan?). A number of good children's atlases are available. Three of the best are *The Eyewitness Atlas of the World* (Dorling Kindersley), *Facts on File Children's Atlas* (Facts on File), and *The Picture Atlas of the World* (Discovery Toys).

➤ Invite your child to use blocks, boards, the garden hose, or anything else he can find to construct a maze for his guinea pig or model race car—or for you to find your way through.

➤ Show your child how to make different kinds of graphs to record surveys.

Most Hated Vegetables in Our Class

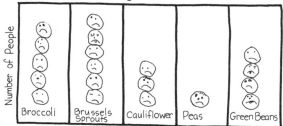

Most Hated Vegetables in Our Class

Most Hated Vegetables in Our Class

➤ The computer is a wonderful learning tool for children at any stage of learning, but it is especially useful for the practice, practice, practice that makes up so much of elementary mathematics. A number of fine books are available that review children's software. Look for these and others in your library:

• *The Best Toys, Books, Videos and Software for Kids 1997: 1000 + Kid-tested Classic and New Products for Ages 0-10,* by Joanne Oppenheim

- *The Family PC Software Buyers Guide,* by Kurt Carlson (Valle Dwight)
- *Kidware: The Parent's Software Guide, Vol. 1* by Michael C. Perkins (Celia Nunez)
- *Home Education Resource Guide,* by Cheryl Gordon

➤Guess what? Your misspent youth was not for naught. This is the age when your child can begin to figure out those tavern puzzles that you spent so many hours puzzling over so long ago. Books of math puzzles often include matchstick and other tavern puzzles. Here are a couple to remind you of the good old days. (Just in case you need them, the solutions are on page 183).

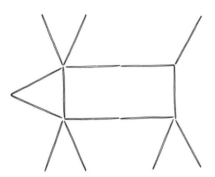

Look at this deer made of toothpicks. Move two toothpicks so that the deer is facing the opposite direction.

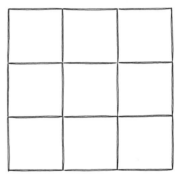

Count these squares (9). Can you take away 8 sticks and leave only 2 squares?

➤Most second graders are puzzle hounds, and second graders who love math are the most enthusiastic of the lot. Although there are many books of mathematical puzzles on the market, few are geared toward younger children. Try *Number Mysteries* by Cyril Hayes and Dympna Hayes (CHP Books), or ask your librarian for suggestions.

Working with Your Child's Teacher

This book and the accompanying assessment can provide you with lots of information about second grade expectations and how your own child is progressing toward meeting those expectations. There is, however, much information about your child's schooling that this book cannot provide.

This book cannot tell you, for example, the methods your child's teacher uses to teach second grade skills. The book also cannot tell you the sequence in which the skills will be taught or integrated into the curriculum. No book can tell you exactly how your child's performance is being measured and recorded this year, since assessment methods vary greatly from school to school and from classroom to classroom. Nor can any book give you a clear picture of how your child interacts in the classroom (you may discover that your child can behave quite differently in a different setting) or how your child is doing socially.

To gather this kind of information you must form a strong line of communication with your child's teacher. Most schools provide several ways for teachers and parents to share information, but you may discover that you will glean far more information if you take the lead now and then. Here are some ways that you get a closer look at your child's learning experience.

Open House

Open house, also known as parents' night or back-to-school night, is an evening set aside for teachers to present to parents their goals, methods of instruction, and routines. The purpose of this event is not to discuss individual students but to introduce the program and classroom procedures as a whole.

Open house presentations are as varied as the personalities of teachers who give them. Your child's teacher may present you with a brief written description of his expectations, or he may simply invite you to come into the room and look around. He may have you participate in some of the math and reading activities that the children do, or he may even prepare a video or a slide show to demonstrate a typical day in second grade.

If your child's teacher has not prepared an elaborate or particularly detailed presentation, do remember that not all teachers are extroverts. Many feel far more comfortable in a room with twenty-five rambunctious seven-year-olds than in front of a group of adults. If this is true of your child's teacher, try posing a few encouraging questions to help the teacher provide you and other appreciative parents with more detailed information.

"But," you might say, "what if I am not an extrovert either? And besides, I don't want the teacher to think I'm an overbearing or uncooperative parent." Indeed, many parents find that they are more anxious on parents' night than the teachers are. The parents' own experiences as students or their lingering fear of authority may cause trepidation. After all, whose heart doesn't beat a little faster at the thought of being sent to the principal's office? Simply meeting the person with whom your child will spend over 180 days this year can be unnerving enough to cause you to sit passively at your child's desk.

Keep in mind that *how* you pose your questions can make a difference. Questions need not be challenges. They can be invitations. "What do land forms have to do with addition and subtraction?" is a challenge. "Your study of land forms sounds fascinating. Can you tell us more about how you will integrate math skills into that study?" on the other hand, is an invitation to discussion. Most teachers are passionate about children and about the subjects they teach. Encourage your child's teacher to expound on what excites him most.

Parent Conferences

There are three kinds of parent-teacher conferences: regularly scheduled conferences, special conferences that you initiate, and special conferences that your teacher initiates. The purpose of each of these conferences is the same: to discuss how your child is doing and how you can support him emotionally and educationally. Your role in each of these conferences, however, may vary depending upon who initiated the conference.

Scheduled Conferences

Scheduled conferences usually occur once at the beginning of the school year and once later on in the year. Before you attend a scheduled conference, you'll want to gather some data. Remember, the more information you have going into a conference, the easier the conference will be for everyone. Begin with your child. Long before the conference time, you should be asking specific questions. "How's school going?" may not elicit much of a response. However, specific questions, such as those below, might prompt a more meaningful response:

- What books are you reading in school?
- What's your favorite thing to do in class? Why?
- What do you like best (or least) about math?
- Does your teacher call on you very often?
- What worries you about school?

As you prepare the questions you wish to ask your child's teacher, be aware that the teacher herself is preparing to meet with more than twenty sets of parents. It is likely that she has established a routine, such as showing you samples of your child's work or the results of formal and informal assessments. She may have one or two issues she wishes to bring to your attention. Because of the uniformity of these conferences, you might find yourself wondering if the teacher truly knows your child. A comment such as "Your son is such a pleasure to have in class" is nice to hear. But it is not nearly as useful—and ultimately as cherished—as "Your son has read all of the beginning mysteries in the classroom and is now gobbling up books about space." To elicit more specific comments about your child, feel free to ask questions like these:

- In what areas have you seen the most growth? The least?
- How does my child's performance compare with that of other children at this grade level? Teachers understandably do not like to compare children and are often reluctant to answer this question, but it is an important one. Keep in mind that you need to know about your child's progress and performance. The teacher may tell you that your child is growing daily as a reader. However, until you know that that growth is taking place in the lowest reading group, you only have half of the picture.
- What are my child's work habits like?
- What are my child's interests?
- What motivates my child in school?
- Does my child have any special friends? What are they like?

- How would you describe my child's attention span?
- What can I do at home to support my child's learning?

If during the conference the teacher uses jargon you're not familiar with or if the teacher describes your child in ways that seem vague, ask for clarification. "A live wire" could mean that your child is bright and curious or that he has difficulty sitting still or paying attention. Try not to leave the conference until you are sure you have a clear picture.

Most routine conferences are scheduled in fifteen- to twenty-minute blocks (which is why you want to be on time for yours). If your conference is coming to an end and you have just unearthed an area of concern, ask to schedule another conference. Most teachers will be happy to do so.

You may find that your child is invited or expected to attend your teacher's conference with you. This format has both advantages and disadvantages. By attending the conference, your child will be encouraged to take a more active role in his own learning and assessment. You, however, may have questions you would like to discuss with the teacher privately. If your child has been asked to attend and you do not want to discuss all of your concerns in his presence, request a second conference time or indicate that you will be following up with a phone call.

When You Initiate a Conference

Although you may be tempted to seek information from the teacher during a class field trip or while you're dropping your child off at school after a dentist appointment, try to refrain from doing so. Impromptu discussions about one child's progress are too much to ask of a teacher who's fully immersed in teaching. Instead, if you have concerns or wish to know more about your child's learning, make an appointment to see the teacher or speak with her on the telephone.

You may want to schedule a conference or phone call to inform the teacher of any stresses or special circumstances your child is experiencing. Illness, parental separation or divorce, death of a dear one (including pets), and particular fears can all affect a child's school experience and are well worth revealing to the teacher. It is also appropriate to schedule a conference if you have noticed confusing or unwarranted changes in your child's behavior. Together you and the teacher may be able to pull together enough information to make sense of the change.

At times, your concerns may have less to do with your child's individual progress than with the classroom situation as a whole. Perhaps you take issue with a specific method your child's teacher is using, or you would like to see learning addressed in other ways. Parents often hesitate to talk to teachers about these considerations for fear that the teacher will feel attacked and subsequently take her anger out on their child. This common fear is rarely warranted. Teachers know that listening and responding to parents will ultimately bring about more support, not less. In most situations a concern, particularly a first-time concern, is taken quite seriously, especially if your choice of words and tone of voice are cooperative rather than confrontational. In schools, as in other institutions, the squeaky wheel does get the grease. Scheduling a conference and expressing your concern in a genuine spirit of collaboration is appropriate.

If you have a concern about your child and are wondering if you should set up a conference, do so, and do it *now*. (October is not too soon.) It is far better to communicate early, when both you and your child's teacher can be proactive rather than reactive. Address the problem *before* your child experiences frustration or a sense of failure. Success is the leading motivator in school achievement. Don't let your child lose that feeling of success.

When the Teacher Initiates a Conference

Suppose you come home from work to find a message on your answering machine: your child's teacher wants to have a conference. Like any parent, you assume the worst. First comes the flood of questions for your child: "How are things going at school? Any problems?" Next comes the steady flow of parental guilt: "What have I failed to do?"

Don't panic. Find out the specific purpose of the meeting. Who knows? Your child's teacher may simply want to talk to you about a volunteer position in the classroom or about your child's special talents. If she seems reluctant to give you details before a meeting, understand that this is to prevent an immediate and full-range discussion at the time of the phone call. In truth, it is probably more advantageous for everyone involved to wait, process the information, and be prepared at the meeting. To find out the purpose of the meeting, you might say, "I know that we don't have time to discuss the issue now, but could you tell me in a few words what the conference will be about?" Then ask who, other than the teacher, will attend the conference. Finally, ask, "Is there a helpful way that I can prepare?" This last question will set the right tone, indicating that you are open and eager to work together.

Whether you initiate a conference or the teacher does, remember that the main purpose of any conference is to collect and share essential information. More often than not, teachers are relieved when parents bring problems to their attention. You, too, should be glad that a problem has been noticed and addressed. At the very least, by opening a vital line of communication, you and the teacher will clarify important views pertaining to the education of your child.

Student Assessment

When you went to school there were probably two types of assessments: tests and report cards. The same holds true for many schools today. In some schools, primary students do not take tests, except perhaps for a weekly spelling test, but they do get report cards. The report card may have letter grades; it may be a checklist; or it may be an anecdotal report. In still other schools new methods of evaluation, called performance-based testing or authentic assessment, use anecdotal records, learning journals, and portfolios as a means of reporting progress. A third type of assessment is the standardized test. These types of assessment look at learning from one or more angles, and all can be helpful to you and your child if you understand the benefits and limitations of each form.

Report Cards

Report cards are often considered a conclusion: How well did your child do this quarter? How hard did she try? Many types of report cards, however, raise more questions than they answer. If your child gets grades, you may find yourself wondering what a B really means. Is your child performing slightly above average for the whole class? Or is your child performing slightly above average in her math group? Can a child in the lowest math group get a B? If your child doesn't get traditional letter grades, but receives an O for Outstanding, S for Satisfactory, and an N for Needs improvement, you may still be left wondering what constitutes an outstanding grade as opposed to a satisfactory grade.

Some schools are moving toward more informative report cards. These usually include a checklist of skills and learning behaviors and are marked according to how often your child exhibits those behaviors (Consistently, Most of the Time, Sometimes, Not Yet). The checklist may also be accompanied by anecdotal records. Remember, the perfect reporting device for all children has yet to be devised. Report cards are designed for parents, so if the reports in your district do not meet your needs, let the principal know.

No matter what type of report card your child receives, try to use it as a springboard rather than as a conclusion. As a springboard, a report card gives you the opportunity to talk with your child. Here are some suggestions:

- Ask your child what she thinks of this progress report. Listen to her feelings and guide her in assessing how well she thinks she's doing.
- First and foremost, praise your child for things done well. In fact, you may want to concentrate only on the positive in your first reaction to a report card.
- If you and your child can see a place that needs improvement, talk about *how* your child could go about improving. Telling him to try harder and giving him incentives (a dollar for every A) are probably not helpful. He

cannot improve without a clear understanding of what is expected of him and how he can work on the problem. If you have already pinpointed a need using the assessment in this book, the report card can provide an opportunity to reinforce the good work you have already begun to do together.

- If you have questions about the report card, or if you need further clarification, schedule a conference with your child's teacher.

Above all, keep your discussion with your child as upbeat and positive as possible. Remember, report cards can tear down what your child needs most: confidence. So as your child's main coach, review the report card, but don't let it define her or give her the impression that your love or respect is based on her ability. Your child is not an A or a C student. She is what we all are, a continuous learner.

Performance-Based Assessment

In many schools, teachers are pushing for changes in assessment. They realize that learning does not occur only at the end of a unit or the end of a marking period; it is happening all the time. In these schools teachers are keeping records while observing children at work. They talk to children about what they know and how they approach problems. In addition, both students and their teachers often save the work that demonstrates learning and keep it in a portfolio.

A portfolio is a collection of work. It may contain several writing samples (usually the rough drafts in addition to the finished product, to show growth), charts and descriptions that show how a child approached a math or science project, drawings or other artwork, and a report or project done over time. Sometimes the teacher chooses what will go into the portfolio, sometimes the child decides and sometimes they select the work together. In any case, the student is usually asked to do some self-assessment.

Most parents find that portfolios are a good source of information about their child's progress and school expectations. They are able to see the quality of their child's thinking, the effort that was applied, and the outcomes. While reviewing a portfolio, parents and teachers can discuss future goals for the child.

Standardized Testing

Standardized tests can be administered to children as early as kindergarten. However, the validity of the tests are less reliable in the early primary grades. Young children are inexperienced in taking tests. They have difficulty following directions and predicting correct test responses. Some schools give practice tests in kindergarten or in grade one or two. Other schools wait until the second or third grade before having children participate in standardized testing.

Standardized tests are considered objective because they are administered in the same manner, with the same directions, to children at the same grade level all across the country. They measure student performance in norms, percentiles, and stanines that allow children to be compared to other children, and schools to be compared with other schools. The results of standardized tests can be used, and are used, in a number of different ways: to determine the strengths and weaknesses of the educational program; to inform teachers and parents about the academic growth of individual students; and to identify children who may have learning problems or who may need a more challenging school experience. (Standardized test scores are often used to select children who need additional support at either end of the learning continuum.)

If your child will participate in standardized testing this year, prepare her by briefly discussing the purpose of the test in a low-key manner—"to help your teacher decide what to teach next and to help your teacher teach you well"—and by making sure that your child has plenty of sleep the night before the test and a good breakfast on test day. It's in your child's best interest not to put too much emotional weight on the test or the test results. If you are anxious, you will likely convey that anxiety to your child, and any undue tension can hinder test performance.

Most schools that use standardized testing send the results to the students' parents. When you receive your child's scores, read the directions carefully to learn how to interpret them. If you have questions about the different numbers, ask the school principal to explain them. Don't be embarrassed or intimidated. Teachers often get a crash course in deciphering the code each year.

If your school doesn't send the results home, and you would like to know how your child fared, call the principal as well. If the test booklet becomes part of your child's school records, you are permitted by law to view it.

You may feel that the results accurately reflect what you know about your child. However, if you feel that there is a discrepancy between how your child performs in the classroom and how she performed on the test, speak to your child's teacher. Ask whether the results of the test are consistent with your child's performance. Keep in mind that many circumstances can affect test results. If your child didn't feel well, was unable to concentrate, or incorrectly interpreted the directions, the test results will not be valid. If the teacher agrees that the test results are grossly inconsistent, and if the test results will affect your child's education—determining her reading or math group, for instance—you may request that your child take the test again. Testing companies can and will provide alternative tests.

Standardized tests can be useful to schools, teachers, and parents, but they can also be misused. Sometimes this limited—and flawed—form of measurement is used to determine whether a child should be promoted or retained, whether a child qualifies for special services, whether a teacher is successful, and whether a school system deserves to receive funds. But a standardized test should never be the sole basis of an important educational decision—particularly one that will affect individual children. Observational data and the assessment of the child's teacher, the parents, and any relevant specialists should also be considered.

Observing Your Child in the Classroom

If possible, volunteer to help out in your child's classroom on a regular basis. Being a regular visitor will allow you, your child's teacher, and your child to relax into normal behavior. Take your cues from the teacher, and try not to offer suggestions too often. Let the teacher know how much you enjoy being in the classroom. If a concern arises, schedule a conference to talk with the teacher just as you would if you were not working side by side.

Even if you can't come into school once a week, offer to go along on a field trip or to help out with a special project. As you work with your child's classmates, you will discover a great deal about how children learn at this grade level, and you'll understand more about the academic goals. Your child will see firsthand how much you value education. His pride in your participation will go a long way toward helping him succeed in school.

Solutions to tavern puzzles:

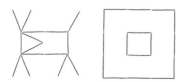

Index

even and odd, 44, 125–26
games with, 126–27,
128–30, 134–37, 141–42
multiplication and division
of, 59, 60, 65, 165–67
ordinal, 59, 125
Roman, 171
rounding off of, 132
strategies with, 133–34,
137–42
ten-based system of,
127–29
two-digit, 18, 61, 127
writing of, 25
0–99 grid of, 191
number sense, 59, 60, 61, 62,
65, 123–27, 131

O

observational assessment,
31–34
see also math assessment;
reading assessment;
writing assessment
organization, 118

P

painting, 25
parent observation pages, 18,
32, 35–54, 65
parents:
children's relationships
with, 21, 22, 29
classroom visits of, 27, 176,
183
emotional and educational
support by, 17–19, 22–27,
29, 31–32, 65, 71
as first and best teachers,
17–18, 71
as learners, 19, 31, 32
questions for children from,
18–19, 28, 31, 34
reading aloud by, 29, 67–71,
77–78, 82–83, 102, 109,
111
reading habits of, 71, 103
school volunteer work of,
179, 183
teacher interaction and
partnership with, 18, 25,
28, 29, 33, 175–83
time investment of, 33
parent-teacher conferences,
176–79
patterns, 97, 125

of counters, 42, 44–45, 59,
60
place value, 192
poetry, 116
prediction and, 99
repetition of, 73
pediatricians, 25, 31
peer relations, 21, 22, 23–24,
26, 118
pencils, 22, 115
pen pals, 121
perfectionism, 24, 28, 84, 110
perseverance, 21, 24
pets, 22
phonics, 66
activities in, 56, 57, 58
consonant sounds and,
85–87
reading assessment and,
56–57, 58, 83
reading exercises and,
83–92
sounding out in, 27, 36, 37,
39, 40, 55–58, 66, 83–92
phrase cards, 100, 190
physical education, 19
pictures:
dictionaries of, 112
drawing of, 30, 115
fractions in, 50–51, 63–64
reading and, 36, 37, 55, 56,
57, 68–70, 147, 167
place value, 18, 60, 62, 127–30,
191
play:
free, 23, 28, 119
with peers, 22, 24, 33
playground chants, 86
plays, 19, 23, 83, 120
poetry, 41, 71, 96, 111, 116
comprehension of, 36, 38,
56
postcards, 71, 110
posture, 25
praise, 22, 25
prediction, 55, 72–74, 99
preschool children, 22, 73, 105
printing, 81
privacy, 23, 26, 108, 109
problem solving, 162
learning new skills of,
20–21, 60
math, 28, 42–54, 56–65,
123–67, 169
real life, 28, 59, 133, 134–35,
172

punctuation, 24, 54, 66, 85
puns, 119

R

reading:
comprehension of, 27, 36,
38, 39, 41, 55–58, 66–83
creating special place for,
82–83
difficulty with, 25, 32, 56–58
fluency in, 41, 56, 58, 101–3,
117
from left to right, 66
pictures and, 36, 37, 55, 56,
57, 68–70, 147, 167
poetry, 36, 41, 71, 111
practice of, 70, 103
prediction and, 55, 72–74,
99
second-grade curricula in,
19
time allotment for, 24, 29
whisper, 102–3
writing skills and, 65
reading aloud, 102
at bedtime, 68, 78
to children, 67–71, 82–83,
109, 111
with children, 29, 77–78
reading assessment, 18,
36–41, 55–58, 66
phonics and, 56–57, 58, 83
poetry in, 36, 56
segmentation and timing
of, 32
stories in, 37–41
words in, 36–41, 55–58
reading enrichment, 56, 57,
58, 117–22
reading exercises, 66–103, 107
discussion and games as,
69–70, 71, 74–75, 77–83
fluency and, 101–3
phonics and, 83–92
reading aloud and, 67–71,
102
reading comprehension
and, 55–58, 66–83
sight words and, 98–101
vocabulary expansion and,
81–82
word study and, 92–97
recess, 22
record keeping, 140, 181
report cards, 180–81
rhymes, 30, 73, 92, 99, 111

if I were	she said	come with me	I will do it
from him	I love you	you and me	by the way
each one	how are you	what is that	all I have
at the store	go to school	here or there	which one

0-99 Grid

0	1	2	3	4	5	6	7	8	9
10	11	12	13	14	15	16	17	18	19
20	21	22	23	24	25	26	27	28	29
30	31	32	33	34	35	36	37	38	39
40	41	42	43	44	45	46	47	48	49
50	51	52	53	54	55	56	57	58	59
60	61	62	63	64	65	66	67	68	69
70	71	72	73	74	75	76	77	78	79
80	81	82	83	84	85	86	87	88	89
90	91	92	93	94	95	96	97	98	99

Place Value Patterns

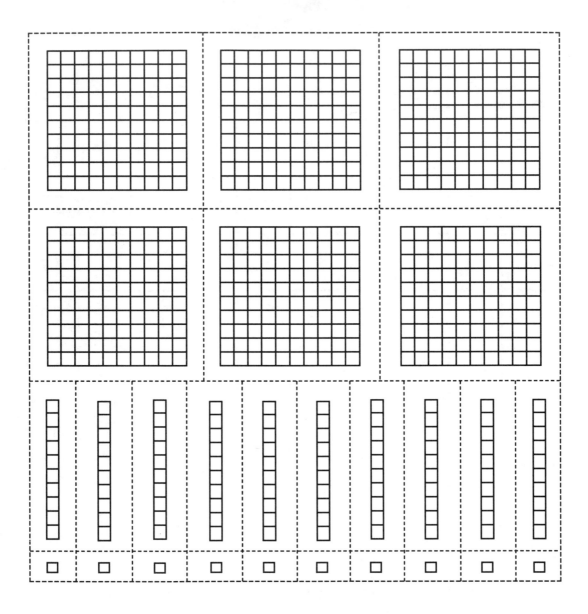